Entrepreneurship in Nebraska

Conditions,
Attitudes,
and Actions

Entrepreneurship in Nebraska

Conditions, Attitudes, and Actions

Eric C. Thompson
Associate Professor of Economics
Director, Bureau of Business Research
University of Nebraska-Lincoln

William B. Walstad
John T. and Mable M. Hay Professor of Economics
University of Nebraska-Lincoln

GALLUP PRESS
New York

Gallup Press
1251 Avenue of the Americas
23rd Floor
New York, NY 10020

Manufactured in the United States of America

First edition 2008

10 9 8 7 6 5 4 3 2 1

ISBN: 978-1-59562-020-0

Contents

Figures

Tables

APPENDIX TABLES

Foreword

Entrepreneurship is a vital and dynamic process that can help Nebraska meet many of its economic goals. It encourages Nebraskans to build an economy that constantly reinvents itself, adapting to new opportunities in a rapidly changing national and global business environment. In both Nebraska's cities and its countryside, entrepreneurship creates new businesses that offer jobs to young people that would not otherwise be available, and it shows them that they do not need to move to another state to achieve success. It allows independent, risk-taking individuals to realize their dreams of being an owner, growing a business, and helping the communities in which they live. Overall, entrepreneurship builds wealth for Nebraska, strengthens our economy, and supports our "good life."

Many Nebraskans recognize the benefits of entrepreneurship and are taking steps to encourage it. I applaud those efforts and have tried to complement them in my own way through my philanthropic and business activities. The Krieger Family Foundation supports a broad range of efforts to stimulate entrepreneurship in Nebraska, such as working with schools to add an entrepreneurship focus to the curriculum, creating a Web site to share information on entrepreneurial activities in the state, and sponsoring research by faculty members at universities. Gallup also supports this emphasis on entrepreneurship in Nebraska. It conducted the two statewide surveys reported in this book, devoted staff time to this project, and co-sponsored the Nebraska Summit on Entrepreneurship with the University of Nebraska. Gallup Press is publishing this book as part of this continuing public service.

The book that Eric Thompson and Bill Walstad have written is an important one to read. They analyze the business and economic conditions affecting entrepreneurship in the state, and they evaluate where we currently stand. Further insights come from extensive investigation of the attitudes and opinions – of the general public and owners of small business – about the state climate for starting new businesses. After all their data reporting, they offer valuable suggestions for actions that can be taken to increase entrepreneurship in Nebraska. Their comprehensive investigation will help us think deeply about what has been accomplished – and what needs to be done – to advance entrepreneurship in the state.

I see new energy building around this statewide goal of enhancing and expanding entrepreneurship. I am excited by this prospect and want it to continue in the coming years. This development means that, going forward, we will need to do a better job of measuring and tracking the level of entrepreneurial activity in the state. We also will need to monitor the climate for entrepreneurship by assessing business and public attitudes, and by evaluating the effects of the tax and regulatory policies of government. This book establishes the foundation and framework for the tracking and monitoring of entrepreneurship in Nebraska that will be needed over time.

The last chapter of the book identifies three areas for action to improve entrepreneurship in the state. The first involves increasing the supply of entrepreneurs through education, both at the pre-college and college levels. The second seeks to expand the ranks of first-time and serial entrepreneurs through the development of innovative methods for finance and technology transfer. The third calls for improving business and economic conditions statewide and in individual communities, so entrepreneurship is actively encouraged and supported. We need to take these actions to remain competitive with other states in the nation. As the authors explain, Nebraska has the potential to become one of the most entrepreneurial states in the nation. Achieving this goal will require much time and effort, but the payoff is enormous for the state's economy, employment, and welfare.

For many years, dedicated individuals in the private and public sectors have worked to increase entrepreneurship in Nebraska. Although much has been accomplished, we now need to be more efficient and effective in our work – and this book will help. I hope this decade marks a renewed effort to make Nebraska an entrepreneurial leader among the states. It has been an important part of my life to build a thriving Nebraska business. I wish that that more young people in Nebraska will have – and will take – the opportunity to do the same.

Jim Krieger
Chief Financial Officer
and Vice Chairman, Gallup

Acknowledgments

We think this book provides a careful investigation of the conditions for entrepreneurship and attitudes about entrepreneurship in Nebraska. The findings for the state overall and for the six community college districts of Nebraska should be useful as a foundation for assessing the current climate for entrepreneurship in the state, and for discussing actions that can be taken to encourage further development of entrepreneurship in Nebraska. Although we think the book has positive features and valuable content, our work in writing the book and its publication would not have been possible without the help and support we received from many individuals.

The inspiration for this book came from Jim Krieger at Gallup who gave us guidance and encouragement throughout this project to understand the conditions and attitudes for entrepreneurship in Nebraska. We could not have completed this work without his leadership for the project, all of the support from Gallup, and the funding from the Jim and Penny Krieger Family Foundation.

We also greatly benefited from the work of Glenn Phelps at Gallup. He helped us prepare the extensive general public and business surveys, oversaw collection of the survey data, and gave us valuable information on survey methods and procedures.

Throughout the project we gained knowledge and understanding from many people in different meetings and venues. Our initial discussions about entrepreneurship in Nebraska began in planning meetings of practitioners and academics that Jim and Glenn convened in summer 2005 at Gallup with Tammi Messman, Louis Pol, Russell Smith, Amy Thomas, Alan Tomkins, Anne York, and other individuals. We also are grateful for the time that others spent with us to discuss actions to support entrepreneurship in Nebraska in personal interviews and informal conversations. The list of people we spoke with includes John Brasch, Gregg Christensen, John Decker, Steve Erwin, Robin Eschliman, Glenn Friendt, Monte Froehlich, Robert Gordman, Bob Harris, Jason Henderson, Peter Katt, and Tim Mittan.

The University of Nebraska played a key role in the development of this book. The 2006 Summit on Entrepreneurship organized by the University provided us with an opportunity to present our first year of findings on conditions and attitudes for entrepreneurship in Nebraska. We received many thoughtful comments and suggestions from the participants at the Summit that helped us expand our research in new directions. We thank President J.B. Milliken of the University of Nebraska and Pete Kotsiopulos, Vice President for University Affairs, who were the driving force in planning the Summit. We also appreciate the encouragement from Cynthia Milligan, Dean of the College of Business at the University of Nebraska-Lincoln, for our presentations at the Summit and for the preparation of this book.

The publication of this book required timely work from a production team at the Gallup Press. We received helpful management and editorial direction from Piotr Juszkiewicz and Larry Emond, careful proofreading from Alyssa Yell, and good design work by Brian Pope. Sharon Nemeth at the University of Nebraska-Lincoln did a superb job in preparing chapters, tables, and pages of the manuscript.

We are most grateful for all of the above contributions, but it should be stated that none of the above individuals are responsible for the findings and opinions presented in the book. They are our own. We alone are responsible for any errors or omissions.

Finally, we view this book not as a final work, but as the first step in a longer research project. We welcome ideas or comments from readers for what we hope or anticipate will be a revision of this book. We think there are significant current developments to be reported about entrepreneurship in Nebraska, and we expect there will be exciting new ones in the future.

Eric C. Thompson

William B. Walstad

CHAPTER 1

Promise and Challenge

Entrepreneurship is of vital importance to Nebraska for many reasons. The creation of new businesses contributes to economic growth in communities across the state as these new businesses become successful and prosper. This economic activity results in the development of new products, services, or technologies that enhance and expand the business and social vitality of the state. As new businesses grow and prosper, they create greater employment opportunities for workers, offer jobs with more variety and diversity for the workforce, and ultimately increase wage and salary incomes for workers.

The many benefits of entrepreneurship from economic growth, increased employment, and greater incomes in turn enrich the tax base for the state and its local communities. The additional tax revenue helps local governments and state government meet their basic needs for infrastructure in the form of new and improved highways, bridges, buildings, or other structures. More tax revenue also helps local and state officials provide other public goods and services such as health care, education, social welfare, and parks and recreation, which are desired by citizens in communities across the state. Of course, more tax revenue is not the intended target from the expansion of entrepreneurship, but nonetheless the public sector as well as the private sector of an economy benefits from a more vibrant and entrepreneurial economy.

The formation and success of new businesses in Nebraska contribute to the welfare of the state in other ways that often are overlooked.

Entrepreneurship has the power to create significant wealth for the founders and owners of businesses, and for investors in those businesses. Some of this wealth then gets returned to local communities across the state through philanthropy. In fact, a substantial amount of private philanthropy comes from the generosity of entrepreneurs who give back to a community with contributions for charitable or educational purposes, or by establishing non-profit foundations to provide a long-term and systematic method for giving to worthy activities and improving communities. In addition, successful entrepreneurs, and many of their employees, often assume leadership roles in charitable and civic activities in their local communities to foster economic development and offer public service.

The many direct and indirect benefits from entrepreneurship to a state's economy and local communities make it a worthy topic for further scholarly study. This book, therefore, considers the vital role of entrepreneurship in the Nebraska economy. The investigation offers a broad perspective. It considers the business and economic conditions in the state that affect the entrepreneurial climate and activity in both the short run and long run. It surveys the opinions and perceptions of entrepreneurs and the general public in Nebraska to discover what each group thinks about such topics as business ownership, entrepreneurship education, government activity, and economic development. It studies entrepreneurial activity and attitudes across age groups and in different regions of Nebraska.

The general purpose of this study is to supply an in-depth understanding of the entrepreneurial climate in the state, and then to suggest some actions that can be taken to improve it. As will be described in more detail throughout the book, Nebraska is an entrepreneurial state in many varied and important ways. There is great interest in and support for entrepreneurship, and participation in new venture creation is high. Nevertheless, Nebraska is an entrepreneurial state within an entrepreneurial nation. There are ways in which entrepreneurship in Nebraska lags such activity in other states, so new means must be found to improve the climate for business formation and increase the level of entrepreneurial activity to keep the Nebraska economy vital and competitive.[1]

MARKETS, LOCATIONS, AND ENTREPRENEURSHIP

The relationship between entrepreneurship and the market economy is a close one. Entrepreneurs benefit from the freedom, self-reliance, and opportunity to build wealth that accompanies business ownership. In addition, society benefits from the efforts of entrepreneurs. Entrepreneurs play a central role in the economy by combining the economic resources of land, labor, and capital to produce goods and services that have value. By focusing on their own enterprises, these businesspeople elevate the national standard of living by continually identifying new markets and ways to serve existing customers at a lower cost. Young businesses in particular play a key role in renewing and growing the U.S. economy through new products, locations, and innovative technologies either to compete with existing firms or expand the economy in new directions. The efforts raise the productivity of the national economy and national income.[2]

Entrepreneurship can provide a comparative advantage to state and local economies. More entrepreneurial areas or locations more quickly expand existing industry clusters and may be more adept at adopting new technologies. Innovative firms are frequently part of existing local industry clusters, and new firms are innovative in less established and niche markets within these industries, thereby generating new income opportunities not seized on by existing firms.[3] More entrepreneurial places also may specialize in emerging industries. For example, the most innovative and high-growth industries, such as electronic components and communications equipment, are also the industries with the highest share of new firms.[4]

The implication is that more entrepreneurial state and local economies may be faster-growing economies. This notion has been supported by the research that found higher levels of entrepreneurship associated with faster growth in regional economies.[5] This positive association between entrepreneurship and growth may be because young establishments exhibit higher average net employment growth rates.[6]

Although entrepreneurship is often associated with innovative industries and urban areas such as Boston, Massachusetts; Austin, Texas; the Research Triangle of Raleigh, Durham, and Chapel Hill, North Carolina; and the Silicon Valley area in California, the fact is that entrepreneurship influences growth in all types of industries and local economies. Research studies have found entrepreneurship to be valuable in both metropolitan and non-metropolitan labor market areas throughout the nation.[7] New business formation occurs in many varied locales and communities within states. Participation in the entrepreneurial economy is not dependent on proximity to certain cities or locations within the country.

What these results imply is that states such as Nebraska, with its large rural population and smaller metropolitan areas relative to other cities, also can be an entrepreneurial place. The potential for a high level of entrepreneurship is certainly present in Nebraska, but it is essentially an empirical question as to whether Nebraska is an entrepreneurial state. To answer the question, researchers must gather and examine a variety of evidence and data on business formation rates in Nebraska, the nature and earnings of new businesses, and the level of interest in and knowledge about entrepreneurship among its population.

As stated previously, Nebraska is becoming a more entrepreneurial state. The initial evidence to support this statement comes from one of the more intuitive and direct measures of entrepreneurship, which is the percentage of all jobs that are held by proprietors. The measure is precisely defined as the number of non-farm proprietors divided by total non-farm employment.[8]

Table 1.1 shows proprietor's share of total employment in both Nebraska and the United States. Proprietor employment is a count of both sole-proprietors as well as the number of proprietors (i.e., partners) involved in business partnerships. The measure of total employment includes both proprietor employment plus wage and salary employment. The data are presented from 1990 to 2005, the most recent year for which the data were available. This fifteen-year period is generally considered a relatively strong period for economic growth in Nebraska; a time where both employment and population were increasing.

Table 1.1:   Non-Farm Proprietor Employment as a Share of Total Employment, 1990–2005

Area	Year			Average Annual Change	
	1990	**2000**	**2005**	**1990–2005**	**2000–2005**
Nebraska	0.142	0.146	0.157	0.0002	0.0021
United States	0.140	0.153	0.173	0.0009	0.0040

Source: U.S. Department of Commerce, Regional Economic Information System.

In 1990, proprietors accounted for approximately 14.0 percent of total employment in Nebraska and in the United States. The share of proprietor employment rose in the decades that followed, increasing to 15.7 percent in Nebraska by 2005 and 17.3 percent nationwide. Thus, in both Nebraska and the United States, proprietor employment has been growing faster than wage and salary employment, indicating the rising importance of self-employment. The trend also may be accelerating because the share of proprietor employment grew most rapidly after the year 2000.

Nebraska clearly participated in this national trend, but also fell behind the nation, particularly during the 1990s. Nationwide, proprietor employment grew from 14.0 percent to 15.3 percent of total employment during the 1990s. In Nebraska, the share barely increased, changing from 14.2 percent in 1990 to 14.6 percent in 2000. Although the percentage of proprietors was growing in Nebraska during the 1990s, the percentage change was roughly at the same pace as wage and salary employment. After 2000, proprietor employment grew much faster in both Nebraska and nationwide.

The results highlight the promise and challenge facing entrepreneurship in Nebraska. The promise is that Nebraska has participated in the nationwide wave of entrepreneurship. Proprietorships are growing. Growth is even faster for other categories of business such as corporations, and Nebraska entrepreneurs, particularly those in the Omaha region, have been generating rising incomes and wealth. In spite of all this growth, there clearly is a challenge because entrepreneurial activity may not be rising as quickly in Nebraska as it is nationwide.[9]

OVERVIEW

This book investigates the promise of and challenge to entrepreneurship in Nebraska. The detailed findings and suggestions for changes are presented in the next six chapters. No one chapter provides a complete description of entrepreneurial activity or climate in the state or within its regions. The book is meant to read as a whole to gain a broad understanding of the topic. Some chapters supply insights through studies of economic and business conditions in Nebraska that affect the level of new business creation. Other chapters rely on survey analysis to probe attitudes and perceptions affecting the climate for entrepreneurship. A final chapter discusses actions that can be taken in the state and its communities. The multiple perspectives presented in the book should enrich this broad understanding of entrepreneurship in Nebraska.

Time offers a valuable perspective, so it is fitting that Chapter 2 begins with a study of the trends in long-term entrepreneurship in Nebraska during the 1990 to 2006 period. It also reports on the rates of business formation and performance within the six community college districts of the state. The chapter describes three measures of entrepreneurship activity: (1) growth in entrepreneurship; (2) the nature of entrepreneurship, and, (3) general indicators of entrepreneurial activity. Growth in entrepreneurship refers to the increase in the number of businesses in Nebraska over time, and to the new firm formation (or birth) rate. Also considered are changes in ownership structure among corporations, partnerships, and the self-employed.

The pace of business formation, or growth in the number of businesses, is only a partial measure of entrepreneurship. Other key questions are: What types of businesses are being created? Are these new businesses in the rapidly growing, and high-technology, industries? Do these businesses create high income and wealth? To address these questions, indicators are presented on the nature of entrepreneurship in Nebraska. The first issue is the level of activity per business. This issue is analyzed by comparing the revenue per business in Nebraska and the nation, as well as growth in revenue per business. Also examined is income per proprietor. In addition to these general measures of the nature of entrepreneurship, the analysis specifically focuses on entrepreneurship in high-growth and technology-based industries such as computer programming, business consulting, and bio-technology.

General indicators of entrepreneurial activity also are important for measuring that activity. Increasing entrepreneurship in an economy typically generates rising incomes and wealth among employers and employees. Such general indicators include rising per capita incomes and rising income from interest earnings and dividends.

In Chapter 3, the analysis switches from the long run to the short run to identify recent trends in entrepreneurship since 2003. Many of the same indicators of growth and the nature of entrepreneurship are tracked. Also introduced is an aggregate measure of entrepreneurial activity. Five key measures of the growth or nature of entrepreneurship in Nebraska are combined to generate a State Entrepreneurship Index. The index is calculated for all 50 states, which permits a comparison to be made on entrepreneurial performance across the 50 states. The finding for this state index is that in recent years Nebraska has had a below-average ranking in entrepreneurship activity. Nebraska lags several nearby states such as Colorado, Idaho, and Wyoming, and surpasses Iowa. The index can be easily updated and tracked in future years to determine if Nebraska can match, and ultimately exceed, the national average for entrepreneurial activity in states.

The investigation switches in the next three chapters of the book from a study of economic and business conditions in the state to a survey analysis of the attitudinal climate for entrepreneurship in Nebraska. The data for this analysis came from two years' worth of surveys of Nebraskans that were conducted by Gallup. It was supplemented for comparative purpose with the national results from another Gallup survey.

In the fall of 2005, Gallup conducted a survey of a representative state sample of 2,460 members of the general public in Nebraska who were 18 years of age or older to find out their opinions about entrepreneurship and related business and economic issues in Nebraska. The general public survey also was designed so that the findings could be reported with representative samples from the six community college regions in the state. A survey with many of the same questions used for the general public also was administered in 2005 to a representative sample of 555 small business owners in Nebraska who owned business firms that had 100 or fewer employees. The design feature for this survey meant that the results could be analyzed and compared by the size of business firms based on the number of employees (1–10, 11–19, 20–29, and 50–100).

In fall 2006, the surveys were administered again by Gallup using some of the same questions, but adding new ones to address additional topics and concerns related to entrepreneurship that had not been covered in the 2005 surveys. A total of 2,475 members of the general public and 567 business owners were questioned in the 2006 surveying. As with the 2005 surveys, the data collection was designed so that the results could be reported for the general public at the state level and by community college region. The responses from the business owners could be analyzed overall and by the size of the business firms. In addition, the 2005 and 2006 results for Nebraska could be compared for some of the same questions with national findings from a 2002 survey conducted by Gallup for one of the authors of the book.[10] Further details about the survey development, sampling, and methods are described in Chapter 4.

The main purpose of Chapter 4 is to present the survey findings on interest in entrepreneurship, reasons people become entrepreneurs, and obstacles to entrepreneurship. The survey results show that there is a very positive view of entrepreneurship in the state, and that interest in starting a business was highest among young Nebraskans. These findings suggest that there is already a large potential supply of entrepreneurs in the Nebraska economy. These potential entrepreneurs are drawn by a perception that entrepreneurship brings independence and the potential to innovate. Nevertheless, as the chapter explains, there are obstacles to entrepreneurship that need to be overcome, some of which involve improved education.

Chapter 5 focuses the survey analysis on two central ideas, knowledge, and education. Test questions included in the surveys show that the general public in Nebraska has a limited understanding of topics and concepts related to entrepreneurship, but that they are aware of their deficiencies. One avenue for addressing this lack of knowledge is better preparation and education for entrepreneurship. Education, both at the high school and college levels, makes a significant contribution to the decision and willingness to start a business according to small business owners. There also is general agreement among both the general public and small business owners that it is important for schools and colleges to teach students about entrepreneurship and starting a business. If those objectives were achieved, there likely would be more entrepreneurs in the state according to most business owners.

In Chapter 6, extensive survey findings on three other important topics are supplied. The chapter first examines the views of the general public and business owners about government. In most cases, the opinions are negative ones, especially in regard to government regulations and taxes, and how they can adversely affect the climate for entrepreneurship in the state. The second section, by contrast, shows the perceptions of business are very positive and there is awareness and appreciation of what successful entrepreneurs and their businesses contribute to a community. The third and longest section of the chapter discusses the views of the general public and small business owners on the many issues related to economic development.   There is general consensus about the problems that need to be addressed and the need to do more to increase entrepreneurial activity in communities. The survey results also show that a key issue affecting entrepreneurship in Nebraska is the impending retirement of entrepreneurs and the increasing demand for business transitions.

After all the evidence is reviewed and data reporting is finished, attention rightly turns to the general concern about what should be done to increase entrepreneurship and strengthen the entrepreneurial climate in the state and local communities. That topic is the subject of Chapter 7. Many actions can be taken to increase the supply of potential entrepreneurs in Nebraska, encourage the formation of technology-based business in high-growth industries, expand the availability of financial capital, and improve the conditions for entrepreneurship. The responsibility for taking these actions rests with no one individual, group, or organization. They can be taken by businesspeople, community groups, professional organizations, and educators. In some cases, there also is a vital role for government.

Entrepreneurship education is an action to influence the supply of entrepreneurs among a state's existing population; that is, the number of people seriously considering the launching of new ventures. Such actions include efforts to use education to help students at the high school and community college levels develop some of the skills and expertise useful for entrepreneurship so they are more willing to consider entrepreneurship as a career or job alternative.

Another set of actions focuses on targeting "growth" entrepreneurs, particularly in specific segments of the economy. These segments could include emerging national industries such as high-technology and knowledge-intensive industries. University-based technology transfer is also a key strategy for encouraging entrepreneurship in high-growth industries. Access to more financing that is flexible and supportive will be important for success in expanding this type of entrepreneurship. One advantage of angel investing is that angels provide valuable financing at the critical start-up phase of a business and also offer seasoned advice for new entrepreneurs.

Once potential entrepreneurs develop businesses, a new set of concerns come into play related to the business climate. Factors such as taxes, regulation, and quality of life influence how many new businesses become profitable and stay in business, whether successful entrepreneurs become serial entrepreneurs who start additional businesses, and whether businesses will be retained in the state. These concerns call forth several actions that can be taken to improve the entrepreneurship climate, including tax relief, regulatory flexibility, and health insurance pools for the self-employed. A related issue is expanding the available financing for new businesses, which already has been mentioned but is worth repeating.

There is no specific timeline for implementing the actions. Some actions can be taken immediately and others may require more discussion and revision before they are accepted or adopted. What needs to be done, however, is to develop a benchmark to measure progress over the next decade. A key question to be asked in this regard is how many of these actions (or suitable substitutes) have been taken over the last year, or taken over a longer period of time such as five or ten years.

To supplement the monitoring of progress on actions, it would be worthwhile to continue to collect and analyze the evidence and data as reported in Chapter 2 through Chapter 6 of this book. They will be important for measuring entrepreneurial activity to track trends in economic conditions, such as the rate of business formation in Nebraska, or whether Nebraska has improved its rank in the State Entrepreneurship Index. Similarly, surveys of the general public and business owners need to be conducted in future years to reveal whether the general public or business owners in Nebraska have become more interested in entrepreneurship, more understanding of business, and more supportive of an entrepreneurial climate in the state.

This book, therefore, offers an in-depth assessment of the current state of entrepreneurship in Nebraska. The results and findings should serve as a baseline measure to track progress in entrepreneurship in the state in the future. Although the evidence shows that Nebraska is an entrepreneurial state, the unknown finding is whether Nebraska can become a leading entrepreneurial state in the nation. With some vision, leadership, and commitment to action, this outcome is quite reachable and feasible for the state. The benefits from this work, as described at the beginning of the chapter, are substantial and worth seeking. State and regions that expand entrepreneurship now are the ones which will experience more economic growth, increased incomes, and more prosperity over the next few decades as the national economy continues to change and evolve.

NOTES

1. Schramm (2006) explains that entrepreneurship is America's competitive advantage in a world economy, and that it is a resource that needs to be exploited to foster entrepreneurial growth. The same argument for the nation also applies to states such as Nebraska.
2. Haltiwanger and Krizan 1999; Acs and Armington 2004.
3. Almeida 1999.
4. Carlsson 1999.
5. Acs and Armington 2004.
6. Haltiwanger and Krizan 1999.
7. Acs and Armington 2004; Low, Henderson, and Weiler 2005.
8. This statistic is the entrepreneurship "breadth" measure developed by Low, Henderson, and Weiler (2005). In the calculation, total non-farm employment includes both proprietors and wages and salary workers.
9. More discussion of data on entrepreneurial activity will be provided in Chapter 2.
10. Kourilsky and Walstad 2007.

CHAPTER 2

Long-Run Trends in Business Conditions

This chapter measures long-run trends in entrepreneurial activity in the state of Nebraska since the 1990s. The trends in entrepreneurial activity in all businesses are examined by tracking overall growth in the number of businesses, birth rates for businesses, and changes in business receipts and income. The focus is on entrepreneurship in potential "high-growth" industries such as technology industries and manufacturing. Growth in technology-focused industries is assessed by tracking patents in Nebraska and investigating growth in industries such as computer programming, business consulting, and bio-technology. The analysis studies increases in manufacturing activity, and more generally measures progress in Nebraska's "target" industries. The first section of the chapter reports on these trends for the state of Nebraska. The second section reports on the long-term performance in entrepreneurship in the six community college districts in Nebraska.

LONG-RUN INDICATORS FOR NEBRASKA

State and local economies periodically experience short one- or two-year periods of unusually strong growth. During these periods, economic data such as entrepreneurship indicators will be strong, but these brief bursts in the economy may not reflect any long-term strength in the economy or entrepreneurial activity in the state. The same could be said of short-term periods of weakness. For these reasons, the analysis begins with a focus on long-term trends in entrepreneurship indicators in Nebraska, tracking data beginning in the early 1990s through recent years. A comparison of the entrepreneurship performance in Nebraska is made with the United States overall.

Growth in Entrepreneurship

A proprietorship is just one of the organizational types that an entrepreneur might choose for his or her business. An entrepreneur also could choose to start his or her business as a corporation. Still others may choose several organizational types during the lifetimes of their businesses. For example, an entrepreneur may start his or her business as a sole-proprietorship or partnership and later incorporate the business as it grows and develops. This section examines growth in the number of Nebraska businesses, both overall and in these categories. It also reports on growth in the number of corporations, S-corporations, partnerships, and sole-proprietorships to provide insights into the nature of entrepreneurship and the characteristics of entrepreneurs in Nebraska.

The section begins with an analysis of the net annual increase in the number of businesses of all types, regardless of organization. This net figure for all businesses is the number of businesses born each year less the number that die each year. The net increase therefore reflects the ability of entrepreneurs to form new businesses as well as their ability to make their businesses survive throughout the year.

In addition to tracking the total number of businesses, also examined is the growth in the number of businesses by category. The net increase by category reflects the number of businesses that join each category in a year (either by starting-up in that category or switching into it) less the number of businesses that exit the category that year.

Table 2.1 provides counts of the number of businesses in Nebraska by type for the 1994–2004 period. The source for the Nebraska data is the annual *Nebraska Statistics of Income* reports from the Nebraska Department of Revenue. Annual counts are used to calculate net annual increases in the number of businesses in Nebraska. Growth rates in Nebraska are then compared with the national growth rates. The Internal Revenue Service's *Statistics of Income* report is the source for the U.S. comparison data. At this time, the national data are only available through 2004, which is why analysis stops at that year.

Table 2.1: Counts of Non-Farm Corporations, Proprietorships, and Partnerships, 1994–2004

| Category | Tax Year | | | Average Annual Change Nebraska | | U.S. |
	1994	2000	2004	Number 1994–2004	Percent 1994–2004	Percent 1994–2004
Total	149,650	158,251	171,993	2,234	1.4%	2.6%
Non-farm sole-proprietors	110,358	111,651	118,270	791	0.7%	2.2%
Corporations	15,483	14,091	13,741	–174	–1.2%	–1.2%
S-corporations	12,184	17,388	21,868	968	6.0%	5.6%
Partnerships	11,625	15,121	18,114	649	4.5%	5.9%

Sources: Nebraska Department of Revenue, *Nebraska Statistics of Income*; U.S. Internal Revenue Service, *Statistics of Income*.

Results in Table 2.1 indicate that Nebraska added over 2,200 businesses per year from 1994 to 2004, for an annual growth rate of 1.4 percent. For a state with fewer than two million people, this annual increase of 2,200 businesses is certainly a sign of progress. The growth also provides further evidence that Nebraska is part of the national trend where a growing share of the workforce is involved in running a business rather than working for someone else.

The growth rate in Nebraska, however, lags the national growth rate of 2.6 percent per year. Most of the difference appears to result from a slower growth rate among sole-proprietorships. The growth rate in Nebraska is roughly one-third of the national rate.

The slower growth rate in Nebraska is not simply the result of slower population growth in the state. Table 2.2 shows the number of businesses in Nebraska and the United States as a share of population. In 1994, there was a higher share of non-farm businesses per person in Nebraska. By 2004, however, the gap had been closed so that the share of businesses per person was roughly the same in Nebraska and the nation. Again, the key factor was slower growth in the number of sole-proprietorships in Nebraska.

The two tables also reveal an interesting trend in the type of business organization that entrepreneurs select. More and more firms are choosing to operate as an S-corporation or a partnership. This development may in part reflect the changing industrial structure of the national economy. These types of organizations are particularly popular among services, finance, and construction businesses. And, employment opportunities in the United States and Nebraska are moving increasingly towards the services sectors, and the construction industry.

Table 2.2: Per Capita Counts of Nebraska and United States Non-Farm Corporations, Proprietorships, and Partnerships, 1994–2004

	Per Capita Counts			Average Annual Change in Counts	
Nebraska	**1994**	**2000**	**2004**	**1994–2004**	**2000–2004**
Total	0.091	0.092	0.098	0.7%	1.4%
Non-farm sole-proprietors	0.067	0.065	0.067	0.0%	0.8%
Corporations	0.009	0.008	0.008	−1.9%	−1.3%
S-corporations	0.007	0.010	0.012	5.3%	5.2%
Partnerships	0.007	0.009	0.010	3.8%	3.9%
United States					
Total	0.085	0.089	0.097	1.4%	2.2%
Non-farm sole-proprietors	0.063	0.063	0.069	1.0%	2.3%
Corporations	0.009	0.008	0.007	−2.4%	−2.9%
S-corporations	0.008	0.010	0.012	4.4%	4.0%
Partnerships	0.005	0.007	0.009	4.7%	4.2%

Sources: Nebraska Department of Revenue, *Nebraska Statistics of Income*; U.S. Internal Revenue Service, *Statistics of Income*; U.S. Census Bureau.

Data reported in Tables 2.1 and 2.2 reflect a count of all businesses in the state and nation. This data, however, are only available with a lag of several years. Data are not available for either 2005 or 2006. Another potential data source is the Quarterly Census of Employment and Wages (QCEW), which is part of the unemployment insurance program operated by the state and federal government in each state. This program collects data from most non-farm businesses that have employees, whether these are sole-proprietorships, corporations, S-corporations, or partnerships. Thus, the QCEW is a good measure of employer businesses.

While the QCEW data does not capture entrepreneurs who work alone, the data do reflect the performance of entrepreneurs who provide most of the wage and salary jobs in the economy. Another feature of the QCEW is that it provides a count of business establishments rather than firms, so that a multi-location firm is counted more than once.

The main appeal of the QCEW data is that it is timely. The data is available with only a small lag. Data are available at this time for 2005 and for the first three quarters of 2006. Using the QCEW data, it is possible to track the recent progress of entrepreneurs in Nebraska.

Table 2.3 shows the number of employer establishments in Nebraska as measured in the QCEW for selected years from 1994 through 2006. The year

1994 was chosen as the starting period in order to facilitate comparison with the firm counts presented in Tables 2.1 and 2.2. The results, however, presented in Table 2.3 would not be significantly different if the 1990 to 2006 period is used instead.[1]

Table 2.3: Number of Employer Establishments, 1994–2006

| Category | Year | | | | Average Annual Change Nebraska | | U.S. |
| | | | | | Number | Percent | Percent |
	1994	2000	2004	2006[a]	1994–2006	1994–2006	1994–2006
Total	44,591	48,544	51,562	54,048	788	1.6%	2.2%

Note: [a]Estimate is based on first three quarters of 2006.
Source: Nebraska Workforce Development.

In Table 2.3, the number of employer establishments grew at a steady rate of nearly 1.6 percent per year for the 12-year period. However, as with all firms, the growth rate of employer establishments was slower in Nebraska than nationwide. The number of employer establishments nationally grew by 2.2 percent per year.

This 0.6 percent gap between state and national growth rates in employer establishments is similar to differences in population growth during the same period. From 1994 to 2006, population in the United States grew on average 0.5 percent faster each year than in Nebraska. As a result, the rate of growth in employer establishment per capita would be expected to be similar in the state and nation.

Table 2.4 shows the number of employer establishments per person in 1994, 2000, 2004, and 2006. The number of employer establishments per person was higher in Nebraska than nationwide during that period. Employer establishments also grew as a share of population throughout the period in both the state and nation. The annual increase in per capita employer establishments was nearly identical for Nebraska and the United States for 1994 through 2006. The increase also was similar for the 1994 through 2004 period. This result suggests that most of the gap in the growth rates of businesses per capita seen in Table 2.2 were due to the slower growth in sole-proprietorships. Many of the Nebraska businesses without employees would be sole-proprietorships and therefore would not be included in the employer establishment data. Finally, the growth rate in employer establishments per person was similar in recent years. From 2004–2006, the annual rate of growth in Nebraska was slightly more than national growth.

Table 2.4: Per Capita Number of Employer Establishments, 1994–2006

	Per Capita Counts				Average Annual Change in Counts		
	1994	2000	2004	2006[a]	1994–2006	1994–2004	2004–2006
Nebraska	0.027	0.028	0.030	0.031	1.0%	0.8%	1.8%
United States	0.025	0.027	0.028	0.028	1.1%	1.0%	1.6%

Note: [a]Estimate based on first three quarters of 2006.
Source: Bureau of Labor Statistics, Quarterly Census of Employment and Wages.

Tables 2.1 through 2.4 as a group present a mixed picture of business growth in Nebraska in recent years. The rate of growth in employer establishments per person in Nebraska was similar to the national rate. Rates of growth also were similar for corporations and partnerships. These findings held during the 1990s as well as in the current decade.

Where Nebraska lagged the nation was in the formation of sole-proprietorships. And, since sole-proprietorships are the most common type of business organization, this meant that the total number of businesses grew at a much slower rate in Nebraska. Given that employer establishments expanded quickly in Nebraska (see Tables 2.3 and 2.4), this finding probably reflects slower growth in the number of the smallest, non-employer proprietorships rather than the businesses that create jobs for wage and salary workers. The result still provides some evidence that entrepreneurship is expanded at a slower rate in Nebraska over the long run.

Firm Births

Data presented in Tables 2.1 through 2.4 on net increases in business counts reflect changes in both the number of business births and deaths over time. The gross rate of business births, however, is also of interest as a measure of entrepreneurship since it focuses the spotlight on the founding of new businesses.

While data on business births is not as widely available as establishment counts, the U.S. Small Business Administration does track *firm* births at the state level. The source of firm birth data is not Internal Revenue Service data as reported in Tables 2.1 and 2.2. Rather, the source is the Economic Census of the U.S. Census Bureau. Businesses are identified in March of each year allowing the Census Bureau to identify businesses that were founded between March of the previous year and March of the current year. The drawback, therefore, is that the data are not directly comparable to the firm count data presented in Tables 2.1 and 2.4. Still, the firm birth data does provide another perspective on the relative progress of entrepreneurship in Nebraska.

Table 2.5 shows the number of firm births per person in Nebraska and the average for the 50 states over the 1994–2005 period. The number of firm births per person in Nebraska was below the average of the 50 states throughout the period. This provides another indicator that business growth and entrepreneurship has been below average in Nebraska in recent years. However, the firm birth rate has been growing more quickly in Nebraska. Going forward, it will be important to continue to monitor this measure to see whether Nebraska is able to continue to close its gap with the national average.

Table 2.5: Firm Births per Person: Nebraska vs. United States, 1994–2005

	Firm Births per Person			Average Annual Change	
	1994–1995	2000–2001	2004–2005	1994–2005	2000–2005
Nebraska	0.0024	0.0026	0.0029	2.1%	3.3%
United States	0.0032	0.0032	0.0034	0.5%	1.4%

Note: Firm births are measured between the months of March.
Sources: U.S. Small Business Administration; U.S. Census Bureau.

The Nature of Entrepreneurship

The business count figures presented in Table 2.1 through 2.5 do not reveal much about the characteristics of Nebraska entrepreneurs. For example, what were the relative receipts of businesses and the income of proprietors in Nebraska relative to the nation? How has Nebraska fared in terms of innovation? This section addresses these questions by providing data on receipts and income for Nebraska businesses.

Data in Table 2.6 show the receipts per business for the four types of business organizations – corporations, S-corporations, partnerships, and non-farm sole-proprietorships. The receipts per business were used rather than income since income is defined quite differently for each entity under the tax code. The data only run through 2004 since this is the last year for which U.S. statistics of income data is available.

Receipts per business were generally as high as or higher in Nebraska than in the nation for corporations or S-corporations. Receipts per business were lower for partnerships and non-farm sole-proprietors in Nebraska in all years. Receipts per business generally grew at a similar rate in Nebraska as nationwide over the 1994–2004 period, although receipts grew faster for Nebraska partnerships. Overall, the trends in receipts per business indicate that Nebraska entrepreneurs have been successful in generating cash flow relative to national averages.

Table 2.6:   Business Receipts per S-Corporations, Proprietorships, and Partnerships, 1994–2004

	Real (Inflation-Adjusted) Receipts per Business			Average Annual Change in Receipts	
Nebraska	**1994**	**2000**	**2004**	**1994–2004**	**2000–2004**
Corporations	$3,061,989	$4,132,140	$3,659,757	1.8%	–3.0%
S-corporations	$829,943	$728,063	$742,609	–1.1%	0.5%
Partnerships	$188,125	$307,780	$507,297	10.4%	13.3%
Non-farm sole-proprietors	$26,215	$23,360	$21,642	–1.9%	–1.9%
United States					
Corporations	$3,376,497	$4,515,509	$3,955,166	1.6%	–3.3%
S-corporations	$753,724	$734,402	$712,770	–0.6 %	–0.7%
Partnerships	$317,891	$626,201	$585,914	6.3%	–1.6%
Non-farm sole-proprietors[a]	$33,558	$33,114	$29,297	–1.7%	–3.0%

Note: [a]1996 data (the earliest year available). Growth rate based on 1996–2004.
Sources: Nebraska Department of Revenue, *Nebraska Statistics of Income*; U.S. Internal Revenue Service, *Statistics of Income*.

Table 2.7 also provides data on proprietors but using the income of business owners rather than the receipts of their businesses. Note that the proprietor income data in Table 2.7 refer to both sole-proprietors and partners in partnerships. Data were available back through 1990 and up to 2005. Results show that real incomes per proprietor were lower in Nebraska than nationally just as with business receipts. However, in contrast to real

Table 2.7:   Average Real (Inflation-Adjusted) Income of Non-Farm Proprietors, 1990–2005

	Firm Births per Person (March to March)			Average Annual Change in Real Income	
	1990	**2000**	**2005**	**1990–2005**	**2000–2005**
Nebraska	$10,160	$12,270	$12,345	1.3%	0.1%
United States	$13,645	$16,048	$15,460	0.8%	–0.7%

Source: U.S. Department of Commerce, Bureau of Economic Analysis, Regional Economic Information System.

(inflation-adjusted) receipts per *sole*-proprietor, real income per proprietor rose modestly throughout most of the period. Further, growth in Nebraska was faster. Income per proprietor grew at 1.3 percent per year in Nebraska versus 0.8 percent in the United States. This indicator suggests that Nebraska entrepreneurs have been successful in generating income relative to national averages.

High-Growth and Target Industries

Results in Table 2.7 suggested that the average non-farm proprietor earns a modest income. This raises the familiar point that not all new businesses are in high-wage, or in high-growth, industries. The examination of aggregate growth in business counts in Tables 2.1 through 2.5 therefore did not provide a complete analysis of entrepreneurship in Nebraska. There is also a need to track growth in entrepreneurship in the industries with the greatest potential to grow the Nebraska economy. These would include high-wage, high-growth industries, and most types of manufacturing industries. While total manufacturing employment is not growing, growth of manufacturing firms has the potential to grow local economies with high-wage employment, and manufacturing has expanded in many parts of Nebraska in the last decade.

Table 2.8 shows both the concentration and growth of the industries of interest in Nebraska during the 2002–2005 period. The more recent period is used due to the changes in the industry classification system in 2001, which makes comparisons with pre-2001 data difficult. The list falls into three groups: Nebraska target industries, which are industries that have been frequent targets selected by economic development agencies in Nebraska; the second group includes other manufacturing industries; the third list includes the high-wage, high-growth service sectors such as software and Internet-based businesses, and technical and high-skill professional businesses.

As is evident in Table 2.8, Nebraska had fewer establishments per person in many of these key industries in 2005. This result suggests that Nebraska may not have been as entrepreneurial as the nation in these key sectors. Recent growth trends, however, tell a different story. Table 2.8 reveals a relatively strong record of growth among employer establishments of the high-growth industries. Among the target industries, the number of employer establishments grew quickly among trucking firms and warehousing firms. Nebraska expanded the number of employer establishments in most other manufacturing industries from 2001 to 2005. Growth in the number of establishments was especially strong for chemical manufacturers and plastics manufacturers. Nationwide, the number of employer establishments declined in all manufacturing industries during the 2001 to 2005 period.

Table 2.8:   Employer Establishments per Person in High-Growth and Nebraska Target Industries, 2001–2005

Area	NAICS Code	Establishments per Person		Average Annual Change	
		Nebraska	U.S.	Nebraska	U.S.
		2005	2005	2001–2005	2001–2005
Frequent Target Industries					
Truck Transportation	484	0.000890	0.000385	1.3%	0.1%
Warehousing and Storage	493	0.000064	0.000046	3.4%	1.6%
Food Manufacturing	311	0.000196	0.000095	−0.5%	−1.4%
Insurance Carriers	5241	0.000262	0.000134	−0.5%	−0.3%
Other Manufacturing					
Chemical Manufacturing	325	0.000061	0.000052	3.8%	−0.6%
Plastics and Metal Products	326	0.000046	0.000049	3.8%	−2.2%
Fabricated Metal Products	332	0.000152	0.000204	0.1%	−1.3%
Machinery Manufacturing	333	0.000110	0.000106	−0.9%	−3.3%
Computer and Electronic Products	334	0.000043	0.000066	−2.8%	−3.2%
Transportation Equipment	336	0.000050	0.000052	0.9%	−0.9%
Miscellaneous Manufacturing	339	0.000088	0.000110	1.9%	−0.4%
High-Wage, High-Growth Services					
Software Publishers	5112	0.000020	0.000033	0.0%	−3.1%
Internet Publishing and Broadcasting	516	0.000015	0.000011	3.0%	−3.5%
ISPs and Web Search Portals	5181	0.000023	0.000030	−8.5%	−11.6%
Data Processing and Related Services	5182	0.000056	0.000042	−6.4%	−2.1%
Accounting and Bookkeeping	5412	0.000431	0.000402	3.0%	2.8%
Architectural and Engineering Services	5413	0.000322	0.000405	2.6%	1.4%
Computer Systems Design	5415	0.000473	0.000507	2.7%	1.0%
Management and Technical Consulting	5416	0.000393	0.000555	5.5%	4.8%
Scientific Research and Development	5417	0.000057	0.000070	7.7%	1.5%

Source: Bureau of Labor Statistics, Quarterly Census of Employment and Wages.

Among the service industries, the rate of establishment formation in Nebraska significantly exceeded the national average in software publishing, Internet publishing and broadcasting, architecture and engineering, computer systems and design, and scientific research and development. This is further evidence of solid performance in entrepreneurship in high-growth industries. While the overall finding is that Nebraska lags the nation in entrepreneurial activity in these target or high-growth industries, recent trends indicate an improvement in Nebraska's performance. It will be critical to continue to monitor developments in these industries going forward.

Patents

Patents are another key indicator of entrepreneurial potential, particularly in high-growth and technology-based industries. Patent activity also reflects the level of innovation in the economy. Table 2.9 shows that there are just a few hundred Nebraska patents each year. The number of patents rose from 1990 to 2005, although at a slower rate than nationally.

Table 2.9: Number of Nebraska Patents, 1990–2005

| Category | Year | | | Average Annual Change | | U.S. |
| | | | | Nebraska | | |
	1990	2001	2005	Number 1990–2005	Percent 1990–2005	Percent 1990–2005
Total	147	253	205	4	2.2%	3.0%

Source: Statistical Abstract of the United States, "Patents by State."

Table 2.10 shows the number of patents in Nebraska per 1,000 residents and a similar national figure. Even on a per capita basis, Nebraska has had slower growth in the number of patents than the nation. The key statistic, however, is the much lower level of patent activity in Nebraska, which had roughly 40 percent as many patents per person as the nation overall.

Table 2.10: Number of Patents per Thousand Residents, 1990–2005

| Category | Patents per Thousand Residents | | | Average Annual Change | |
	1990	2001	2005	1990–2005	2001–2005
Nebraska	0.093	0.147	0.117	1.5%	−5.7%
United States	0.212	0.346	0.279	1.8%	−5.3%

Source: Statistical Abstract of the United States, "Patents by State."

General Indicators of an Entrepreneurial Economy

An entrepreneurial economy contributes to the standard of living by generating income and wealth as well as new businesses. State trends in per capita income and wealth are therefore indirect measures of entrepreneurship. While growth in personal income cannot be tied solely to entrepreneurship since it also depends on other factors such as rising education levels and labor force participation, an entrepreneurial economy will provide rising per capita incomes and wealth. Therefore, it is useful in an analysis of entrepreneurship to check for progress in these measures.

Figure 2.1 shows trends in per capita income in Nebraska relative to the nation. The results show substantial variability over time. In 1990, per capita income in Nebraska was just 92 percent of the U.S. average. It rose to over 97 percent of the U.S. average in 1996, fell to about 92 percent of the U.S. average in 2000, and then rose again to over 97 percent of the U.S. average in 2003. By 2006, Nebraska stood at 94 percent of the U.S. average. In spite of the variability, the results indicate that per person income grew faster in Nebraska than in the nation during that period. Such increases in relative per capita incomes are compatible with a dynamic and entrepreneurial economy.

Figure 2.1

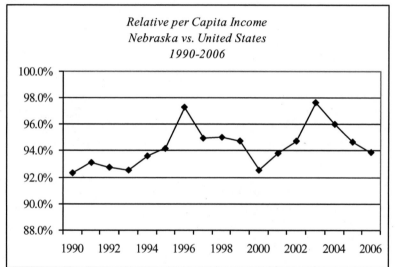

Improvements in per capita income, however, were far from steady. Most of the improvement occurred by 1996. After that year, relative per capita income declined for several years before rising after the year 2000. This irregular pattern is largely due to shifts in income in the volatile farm sector.

To remove the influence of the farm sector, Figure 2.2 presents data on non-farm income per capita in Nebraska and the United States. This figure shows a steady and sustained improvement in per capita income in Nebraska. The magnitude of the increase also was greater. Non-farm income per capita rose from 87 percent of the national average in 1990 to 93 percent of the national average in 2004.

Figure 2.2

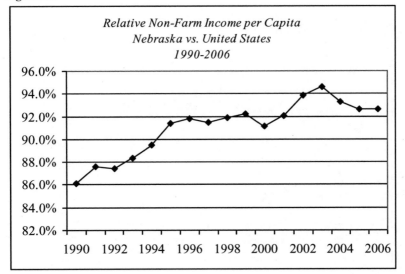

Relative Non-Farm Income per Capita
Nebraska vs. United States
1990-2006

Government data are not available on the aggregate wealth of households in individual states such as Nebraska. There are, however, indirect measures of some components of wealth that are regularly and widely available. One such proxy measure for wealth tracks improvements of income from assets, in particular, income from dividends, interest, and rent. These represent income from interest on bank accounts and certificate of deposits (CDs) and also the dividend portion of income from stocks.[2]

Figure 2.3 tracks the change in the real or inflation-adjusted dividend, interest, and rent income as a proxy for changes in wealth. The figure shows real dividend, interest, and rent income per person in Nebraska and the nation from 1990 to 2006.

Use of per person data adjusts for differences in the growth rate of the population. Nationwide, real income from these sources fell by a few hundred dollars over the sixteen-year period. As might be expected, income from wealth in the United States tended to follow a cyclical pattern, declining during recession and for several years afterwards, and then recovering during the expansion phase of the business cycle. A similar cyclical pattern is seen for the Nebraska series. But, in Nebraska, the long-run trends are positive. There was an increase of several hundred dollars per person. While the Nebraska and U.S. series tracked closely from the early 1990s to 1996, Nebraska outperformed the nation beginning in 1996.

Figure 2.3

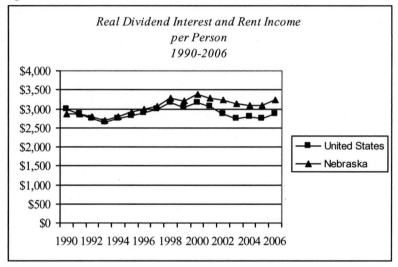

Summary

The statewide analysis of entrepreneurship in Nebraska indicated that Nebraska lagged the nation according to many measures. Despite results for corporations, the overall rate of per capita business formation in Nebraska lagged national averages. This was largely due to a much slower growth in the number of sole-proprietorships. There also is some evidence that Nebraska lagged in terms of innovative businesses, though there have been some recent improvements. Nebraska businesses, however, did have faster growth in real income and receipts than businesses nationwide.

INDICATORS FOR COMMUNITY COLLEGE REGIONS

Nebraska is a diverse state. It includes large and growing metropolitan areas, but also many sparsely populated regions, including regions that have experienced sustained population loss. Patterns of entrepreneurship may vary among these diverse regions. This creates a need for sub-state analysis, since statewide trends may or may not apply to individual regions of the state.

To facilitate sub-state analysis, the state was divided into regions based on the six community college districts of Nebraska. Given the importance of education to the development of entrepreneurs, these districts are natural regions in which to track trends in entrepreneurship. Further, the districts are a fair characterization of Nebraska's diverse economic regions (see Figure 2.4). Two districts each include one of the metropolitan areas of the state. The Metropolitan Community College district includes much of the Omaha area. The Southeast Community College district includes the Lincoln area and the balance of southeast Nebraska.

Figure 2.4

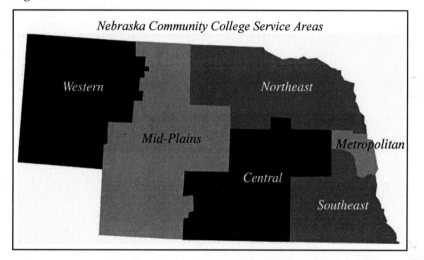

Four other districts reflect the diverse non-metropolitan economies of Nebraska. The Northeast Community College district is home to corn and cattle production, a portion of the Sandhills region, and several manufacturing centers. The Central Community College district includes areas with similar crop production patterns and is populated by the mid-sized tri-cities of Grand Island, Hastings, and Kearney. The Mid-Plains Community College district includes the balance of the sparsely populated Sandhills area and also the cities of North Platte and Ogallala. The Western Community College district includes the western panhandle of Nebraska.

Growth in Entrepreneurship

Statewide analysis of entrepreneurship focused on growth in the number of businesses in Nebraska since the early 1990s. Growth was examined for two typologies. In the first case, business growth was analyzed by type of

organization based on whether businesses were corporations, partnerships, or sole-proprietorships. In the second case, growth was presented for all employer establishments in aggregate, regardless of whether these were partnerships, corporations, or sole-proprietorships. This second typology, however, did not include establishments without employees.

The Nebraska Department of Revenue was the source for statewide counts for corporations, partnerships, and sole-proprietorships. Unfortunately, this data is primarily available at the state level, and is not available for sub-state areas. Therefore, it was not possible to provide analysis on trends in business counts in community college districts using Nebraska Department of Revenue data.

The Department of Labor was the source for the data on employer establishments. This data is available at both the county and state levels. County data can be aggregated in order to develop counts of the number of employer establishments in each community college district. Thus, it is possible to provide analysis on trends in business counts in community college districts using the Department of Labor employer establishment data. Analysis in this section will focus on trends in employer establishments.

Table 2.11 shows trends in the number of employer establishments in each of the six community college districts for 1990 through 2006. It also shows the growth rates for Nebraska overall. Growth rates are repeated for the state since the full 1990–2006 period is being used for sub-state analysis rather than the abridged 1994–2006 period that was utilized previously in Tables 2.3 and 2.4.[3] Establishment counts also are presented for the year 2000, making it possible to distinguish between growth in counts during the 1990s, and growth during the current decade. Counts were rising in both decades.

Table 2.11: Number of Employer Establishments, 1990–2006

Community College District	Year			Average Annual Change	
	1990	2000	2006	Number	Percent
Nebraska Total	39,799	48,544	54,048	891	1.9%
Western CC	2,554	2,692	2,729	11	0.4%
Mid-Plains CC	2,557	2,797	2,952	25	0.9%
Central CC	7,480	8,353	9,089	101	1.2%
Northeast CC	4,036	4,343	4,604	35	0.8%
Metropolitan CC	13,928	17,455	19,416	343	2.1%
Southeast CC	8,730	10,846	12,266	221	2.1%

Note: Districts do not sum to state totals since some establishments are classified as statewide rather than assigned to a particular county. The share not assigned to a particular county has risen over time.
Source: Quarterly Census of Employment and Wages; U.S. Census Bureau.

Growth in the number of employer establishments topped 2 percent in both the Metropolitan and Southeast Community College districts. These rates were somewhat faster than the statewide growth rates. Growth in the number of establishments lagged in the four non-metropolitan community college districts. In three of the four, growth rates for establishment counts were less than half of the statewide growth rate. The growth rate was especially low in the Western Community College district, where the growth rate was about one quarter of the statewide average. Still, it is worth noting that the number of employer establishments did grow in every community college district, including districts such as the Western Community College district where population declined during the 1990–2006 period.

More generally, the pattern for employer establishment growth in Table 2.11 roughly followed the pattern for population growth in the districts, with population growth being the fastest in the Metropolitan and Southeast Community College districts and the slowest in the Western Community College district. While it is true that the stronger rate of firm formation in urban Nebraska may in part explain the faster population growth in these parts of the state, population growth is also influenced by other factors, including preferences for the services and amenities of more urban areas. Thus it is natural to consider trends in the number of employer establishments per person in the community college districts.

Table 2.12 shows establishments per person in each of the six districts for 1990 through 2006. Per person growth rates were strong throughout the state. Growth rates were strong from 1990 to 2000, and then accelerated from 2000 through 2006, particularly in the four non-metropolitan community college districts. The one exception was the Metropolitan Community College district, where the rate of growth decelerated from 2000 through 2006.

Table 2.12: Number of Employer Establishments per Person, 1990–2006

Community College District	Year			Average Annual Change	
	1990	2000	2006	1990–2000	2000–2006
Nebraska Total	0.025	0.028	0.031	1.3%	1.5%
Western CC	0.028	0.030	0.031	0.7%	0.9%
Mid-Plains CC	0.027	0.030	0.032	1.1%	1.3%
Central CC	0.026	0.028	0.030	0.8%	1.3%
Northeast CC	0.026	0.027	0.030	0.9%	1.5%
Metropolitan CC	0.024	0.027	0.027	0.9%	0.6%
Southeast CC	0.023	0.026	0.027	1.2%	1.4%

Sources: Quarterly Census of Employment and Wages; U.S. Census Bureau.

Another interesting result is that the number of establishments per person is highest in the four non-metropolitan districts. This may in part reflect a need for a larger number of small firms to serve a geographically dispersed population in rural areas. For example, in a densely populated urban area a single, larger employer might provide services to 50,000 households, while in a rural area where households are widely dispersed several small firms with just a few employees each might serve the 50,000 households in order to reduce travel costs. Nonetheless, the results still support the presence of significant entrepreneurship in non-metropolitan Nebraska given that Tables 2.11 and 2.12 refer to non-farm establishments. In other words, farm operators, who are some of the most successful and innovative entrepreneurs in non-metropolitan Nebraska, are excluded from the data.

The Nature of Entrepreneurship

Data in Table 2.12 showed that the number of employer establishments per person rose steadily throughout Nebraska from 1990 to 2006. Another issue is whether proprietors were generating rising incomes for Nebraska. Statewide analysis indicated that real (inflation-adjusted) proprietor income grew faster in Nebraska than nationally. A natural question is whether this trend was throughout the state, or whether proprietor income growth was isolated to particular community college districts. Figure 2.5 shows the trend

Figure 2.5

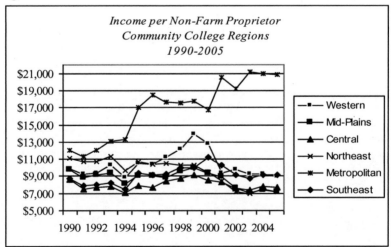

Source: U.S. Bureau of Economic Analysis, Regional Economic Information System.

in real proprietor income in each of the six regions from 1990 to 2005. Data for 2006 is not yet available for counties. The results indicate that it was the Metropolitan Community College district that generated the increase in income per proprietor statewide. Income per non-farm proprietor nearly doubled in the Metropolitan district but was unchanged in the other five districts. Entrepreneurs were creating new businesses throughout Nebraska, but Omaha-area entrepreneurs were most consistently turning entrepreneurial ventures into to high-income operations.

General Indicators of an Entrepreneurial Economy

A similar pattern is evident in data for real per capita income growth and growth in real per capita dividend, interest, and rent income (i.e., income from wealth). Figure 2.6 shows the trends in relative per capita income in the community college districts from 1990 to 2005, the last year for which county income data are available. There was a strong increase in real per capita income in the Metropolitan district, where it grew nearly ten percent faster than nationwide. It declined in most other districts, indicating that income growth did not match national growth rates. The exception was the Southeast district, where relative per capita income rose modestly. For the most part, the strong performance of the Omaha area is what allowed the state to exceed national growth rates in per capita income from 1990 to 2005.

Figure 2.6

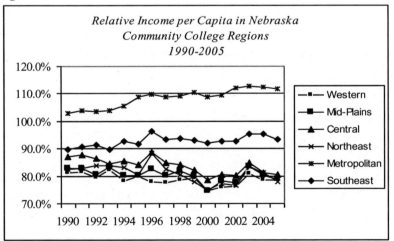

Source: U.S. Bureau of Economic Analysis, Regional Economic Information System.

The case is the same for real per capita dividend, interest, and rent income, which is our proxy for wealth creation. Recall that, statewide, this measure increased in Nebraska while it was stagnant nationally from 1990 to 2006. Figure 2.7 shows trends in real dividend, interest, and rent income per capita for the six community college districts from 1990 to 2005. This measure grew only modestly, if at all, in five of the six community college districts. There was a rapid increase in the Metropolitan Community College district, however, throughout the period. The increase in this district was driving the statewide improvement in this measure of income from wealth.

Figure 2.7

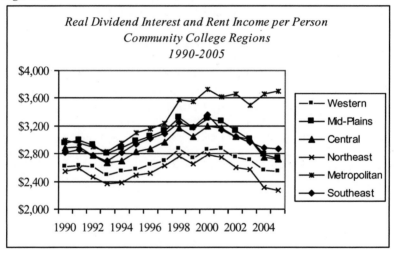

Source: U.S. Bureau of Economic Analysis, Regional Economic Information System.

Summary

Statewide analysis indicated that Nebraska lagged national trends in employer establishment growth, and exceeded national trends in real income per proprietor and in real per capita income growth. This section examined these measures in sub-state regions within Nebraska. The regions were the six community college districts in the state of Nebraska.

Sub-state analysis indicated that the number of employer establishments rose most quickly in the Metropolitan (Omaha) and Southeast Community College districts. However, on a per person basis, the number of establishments expanded at a roughly equal rate in most community college districts of the state. Entrepreneurship was evident throughout Nebraska.

The nature of entrepreneurship, however, appeared to differ in the Metropolitan Community College district. It was Omaha-area entrepreneurs who were most consistently turning entrepreneurial ventures into high-income operations. Real income per non-farm proprietorship rose rapidly in the Metropolitan district, well exceeding national growth rates. Real income per non-farm proprietorship was flat in the other five Nebraska regions, falling short of national growth rates. The same pattern was evident in two other key economic indicators: real per capita income, and real dividend, interest, and rent income per capita. Relative per capita income grew about ten percent in the Metropolitan Community College district from 1990 to 2005, rose one-third as fast in the Southeast Community College district, and was flat or declining in the other four districts. Real dividend, interest, and rent income per capita rose in the Metropolitan Community College district but were flat in all other districts. Thus it was the Omaha area that allowed Nebraska to exceed national trends in terms of growth in income per non-farm proprietor, per capita income, and dividend, interest, and rent income per capita.

CONCLUSION

The United States has experienced a surge in entrepreneurship in the last two decades that has fueled economic growth and innovation. States and regions with an entrepreneurial climate have seen strong growth, wealth creation, and rising incomes. This scenario of entrepreneurial growth in part has also been evident in Nebraska.

Long-run analysis of entrepreneurship in Nebraska indicated that by some measures the state was fully participating in national trends in entrepreneurship. The overall rate of growth in the number of businesses in Nebraska did lag national growth rates, even on a per capita basis. However, this difference was primarily due to slower increases in the number of sole-proprietorships in the state. The number of corporations per capita and the number of partnerships per capita grew as rapidly in Nebraska as nationally. The number of employer establishments per person also grew just as quickly in Nebraska as in the nation. Nebraska also had solid growth in the number of manufacturing establishments, and in the number of establishments in high-wage, high-growth services industries.

Receipts also have grown steadily in Nebraska businesses. Both receipts per business and, in the case of proprietorships, income per business have grown at a faster rate in Nebraska than nationwide. Nebraska also experienced stronger growth in both per capita income and income from wealth than the nation over the past 15 years.

However, Nebraska did lag the nation by some measures. Nebraska had a slower rate of business births than the nation over the last decade. Nebraska also lagged national averages in terms of patents per person.

Long-run analysis in the six community college districts indicated that on a per person basis the number of establishments expanded at a roughly equal rate throughout the state since 1990. This indicates that the population continues to engage in entrepreneurial ventures across Nebraska. The nature of entrepreneurship, however, appeared to differ between the Metropolitan Community College district (Omaha) and the five other community college districts. It was Omaha-area entrepreneurs who generated rapidly growing income per proprietor. Similar long-run trends were seen in terms of income creation. In other words, it is Omaha that most closely fits the scenario of an entrepreneurial economy fueling wealth creation.

NOTES

1. For the 1990–2006 period, the count of employer establishments grew by 1.9 percent per year in Nebraska and 2.3 percent per year nationally.
2. The figure does not reflect an increase in wealth from increases in the value of stocks.
3. The shorter period was used in statewide analysis to facilitate comparisons with Department of Revenue business counts, which were only available back to 1994. However, these data are not available at the sub-state level so there is no reason to utilize the 1994–2006 period.

CHAPTER 3

Recent Trends in Business Conditions

The ultimate motivation for tracking entrepreneurship in Nebraska is to understand where the state stands currently and to monitor its future progress. This chapter again examines entrepreneurship indicators for Nebraska and its six community college districts but now with a focus on recent trends rather than a long-run perspective. The goal is to develop a snapshot of the current progress of entrepreneurship in the state and to provide a series of indicators which can be used to measure changes. The first section of the chapter presents findings on recent growth in entrepreneurship in Nebraska. It is followed by a second section that examines the nature of entrepreneurship. An aggregate index of entrepreneurship is developed and used to benchmark and compare entrepreneurship in Nebraska with other states in the third section. The fourth section reports recent trends in community college districts in Nebraska.

GROWTH IN ENTREPRENEURSHIP

Long-term analysis presented in the last chapter indicated rapid growth in entrepreneurship in Nebraska and the nation beginning in 2000. Data from recent years shows that this trend has continued. As seen in Table 3.1, the number of employer establishments has grown by about 2 percent per year since 2003, with the most rapid growth in 2004–2005.

Table 3.1: Number of Employer Establishments, 2003–2006

	Year				Average Annual Change in Counts		
	2003	2004	2005	2006[a]	2003–2004	2004–2005	2005–2006
Nebraska	51,141	51,562	53,051	54,048	0.8%	2.9%	1.9%
United States	7,963,340	8,093,142	8,294,662	8,515,100	1.6%	2.5%	2.7%

Note: [a]Estimate based on first three quarters of 2006.
Sources: Bureau of Labor Statistics, Quarterly Census of Employment and Wages; Nebraska Workforce Development.

Growth in Nebraska, however, was below the national average in two out of the three years. Nebraska lagged the national average partly because overall economic growth in the state was well below rapidly growing states such as Nevada, Arizona, and Florida. But, as is seen in Appendix 3, Nebraska is closer to the median state. Appendix 3 ranks all states in terms of employer establishment growth. Nebraska was ranked below the median state in two of the three years: ranked 36th from 2003–2004, 15th in 2004–2005, and 30th from 2005–2006. However, Nebraska's average rank for the three years was 27th of 50, quite close to the median.

Table 3.2 shows the number of employer establishments per person from 2003 through 2006. In Nebraska, the number of employer establishments rose from 2.94 per 100 persons in 2003 to 3.06 per person in 2006. This is a significant annual increase, particularly in the past few years. The number of employer establishments per person rose by just 0.2 percent from 2003–2004, but then the rate of growth increased to 2.2 percent from 2004–2005, and 1.3 percent from 2005–2006.

Table 3.2: Per Capita Number of Employer Establishments, 2003–2006

	Per Capita Counts				Average Annual Change in Counts		
	2003	2004	2005	2006[a]	2003–2004	2004–2005	2005–2006
Nebraska	0.0294	0.0295	0.0302	0.0306	0.2%	2.2%	1.3%
United States	0.0274	0.0276	0.0280	0.0284	0.6%	1.5%	1.7%

Note: [a]Estimate based on first three quarters of 2006.
Source: Bureau of Labor Statistics, Quarterly Census of Employment and Wages.

Nebraska's growth rates essentially matched the national average from 2003 to 2006. During this three-year period, the number of employer establishments per person rose by an average of 1.3 percent per year in both Nebraska and the nation.

Taken together, these results show that Nebraska residents were able to match the nation in growth of employer establishments, after adjusting for the slower population growth in the state. However, entrepreneurship is one factor among many that influences the rate of population growth in Nebraska. And the overall growth in employer establishments in Nebraska lagged the nation. This suggests that Nebraska lagged the nation in establishment growth in recent years.

Further evidence of this is provided in Table 3.3, which shows the business birth rate in Nebraska from 2003 to 2005; the data is not yet available for 2006. The number of business births per person in Nebraska is lower than the average for the other 49 states. In fact, the rate in Nebraska is well below the average. This raises the issue of where Nebraska ranks among the 50 states. Appendix Table 3.2a ranks the business birth rates for the 50 states for 2003–2004, and for 2004–2005. Nebraska ranks 30th among states for business births per person during 2003–2004, and 32nd from 2004–2005. Nebraska is slightly below the median state but is not among the lowest ranked states. Among neighboring states, note that Iowa is one of the lowest ranked states in both years, while Wyoming, Montana, and Colorado are among the highest ranked states. Missouri, Kansas, and North Dakota have rankings similar to Nebraska's.

Table 3.3: Firm Births per Person: Nebraska vs. United States, 2003–2005

	Firm Births per Person	
	2003–2004	**2004–2005**
Nebraska	0.0028	0.0029
United States	0.0033	0.0034

Note: Firm births are measured between the months of March.
Sources: U.S. Small Business Administration; U.S. Census Bureau.

NATURE OF ENTREPRENEURSHIP

The status of entrepreneurship in Nebraska depends on the type of businesses created as well as the number. One key issue is the earnings of entrepreneurs in the state. Table 3.4 shows the average real (inflation-adjusted) earnings of proprietors in Nebraska and the United States during the 2003 through 2005 period; the data are not yet available for 2006. Nebraska has lower income per proprietor than the nation and real income also grew more slowly. In Nebraska, real proprietor income grew by 1.6 percent in 2004 and declined by 0.8 percent in 2005. The average annual change from 2003 to 2005 was a modest 0.4 percent. This is well below the average increase of 1.3 percent from 1990 to 2005 (see Table 2.7). Nationally, the average annual increase from 2003 through 2005 was 0.9 percent per year, which is the same as the long-run average from 1990 to 2005. These data are another indicator of a sub-par performance of Nebraska entrepreneurs in recent years.

Table 3.4:   Average   Real   (Inflation-Adjusted)   Income   of   Non-Farm Proprietors, 2003–2005

| | Year | | | Average Annual Change in Real Income | |
	2003	2004	2005	2003–2004	2004–2005
Nebraska	$12,252	$12,443	$12,345	1.6%	−0.8%
United States	$15,179	$15,678	$15,460	3.3%	−1.4%

Source: U.S. Department of Commerce, Bureau of Economic Analysis, Regional Economic Information System.

Table 3.5 shows recent trends in establishment growth among the focus industries: the Nebraska target industries, other manufacturing industries, and high-wage, high-growth service industries from 2003–2005. Recall that in the longer-term analysis, Nebraska lagged the nation in employer establishments per capita in these industries, but had a stronger growth trend. Table 3.5 reveals that the positive growth trends did not continue among the Nebraska target industries in recent years.   Growth rates were similar in Nebraska and the United States in these two periods, except for the insurance industry.   For insurance carriers, the number of establishments per person declined in Nebraska while it grew nationally.

Nebraska did better in the other focus industries. Nebraska outperformed the nation in recent years in other manufacturing. The number of Nebraska establishments grew in several individual manufacturing industries, particularly chemical manufacturers and plastics manufacturers. Nationally, the number of establishments declined in both years in almost all industries. Among the service industries, the rate of establishment formation in Nebraska significantly exceeded the national average in many individual industries including Internet publishing and broadcasting, architecture and engineering, computer systems and design, management and technical services, and scientific research and development. Therefore, positive trends have been sustained in recent years among manufacturing and high-growth, high-wage service industries.

Table 3.5: Employer Establishments per Person in High-Growth and Nebraska Target Industries, 2003–2005

Area	NAICS Code	Nebraska Average Annual Change		United States Average Annual Change	
		2003–2004	2004–2005	2003–2004	2004–2005
Frequent Target Industries					
Truck Transportation	484	–0.7%	2.6%	0.1%	1.9%
Warehousing and Storage	493	1.9%	7.6%	3.1%	2.8%
Food Manufacturing	311	–1.7%	–1.1%	–1.6%	–0.9%
Insurance Carriers	5241	–1.2%	–4.0%	1.3%	–0.3%
Other Manufacturing					
Chemical Manufacturing	325	4.2%	8.0%	–0.4%	0.7%
Plastics and Metal Products	326	8.6%	5.3%	–2.0%	–1.0%
Fabricated Metal Products	332	–3.7%	4.3%	–1.6%	–0.4%
Machinery Manufacturing	333	–1.5%	–1.0%	–3.1%	–2.7%
Computer and Electronic Products	334	–9.1%	7.1%	–3.6%	–0.7%
Transportation Equipment	336	–4.9%	12.8%	–0.4%	–0.2%
Miscellaneous Manufacturing	339	2.0%	0.7%	–0.2%	–0.1%
High-Wage, High-Growth Services					
Software Publishers	5112	–10.5%	2.9%	–4.7%	–0.3%
Internet Publishing and Broadcasting	516	4.2%	8.0%	–1.5%	6.8%
ISPs and Web Search Portals	5181	–2.3%	–7.0%	–11.2%	–7.3%
Data Processing and Related Services	5182	–1.0%	–2.0%	–2.6%	–0.6%
Accounting and Bookkeeping	5412	–2.6%	3.0%	–2.5%	2.0%
Architectural and Engineering Services	5413	–1.0%	9.0%	1.2%	2.1%
Computer Systems Design	5415	3.5%	7.9%	0.2%	3.1%
Management and Technical Consulting	5416	3.9%	12.5%	3.6%	6.9%
Scientific Research and Development	5417	3.3%	7.4%	1.6%	4.0%

Source: Bureau of Labor Statistics, Quarterly Census of Employment and Wages.

Table 3.6 lists patent data for Nebraska and the United States since 2003, as another measure of innovation in the Nebraska economy. The table shows the number of patents in Nebraska per 1,000 residents, and a similar figure for the United States. As was noted earlier, Nebraska is well below the nation in patent activity. For example, the table shows that there were 13.8 patents per 100,000 residents in Nebraska in 2003, versus 33.9 patents per 100,000 residents nationwide in that year. In other words, the number of patents per person was 60 percent less in Nebraska than nationwide. Table 3.6 indicates that the state has not improved its position in terms of patents since 2003. Nebraska has seen a sharp decline in patents per capita, just like the nation as a whole.

Table 3.6: Number of Patents per Thousand Residents, 2003–2005

	Patents per Thousand Residents			Average Annual Change	
	2003	2004	2005	2003–2004	2004–2005
Nebraska	0.138	0.131	0.117	–5.1%	–11.0%
United States	0.339	0.320	0.278	–5.4%	–13.1%

Source: Statistical Abstract of the United States, "Patents by State."

STATE ENTREPRENEURSHIP INDEX

The indicators presented above describe a below-average performance in entrepreneurship in Nebraska over the last few years. It is difficult, however, to interpret the trends in such a diverse set of indicators. To facilitate a more precise aggregate comparison between states, we developed an aggregate entrepreneurship index combining information from many of the tables presented above. The index averages state performance on five measures:

- Percent growth in employer establishments (Tables 3.1 and 3.1a)
- Percent growth in non-farm proprietorships per person (Table 3.5a)
- Business formation rate (Tables 3.3 and 3.2a)
- Real income per non-farm proprietorship (Tables 3.4 and 3.3a)
- Patents per thousand residents (Tables 3.6 and 3.4a)

The first three indicators were chosen to provide a broad-based measure of growth in the number of businesses in the state over time. One measure examines the increase in businesses adjusting for population growth in the state; the other not adjusting for population. One measure focuses on growth in all businesses, the other on the businesses large enough to have employees. One measure examines the formation rate for businesses, while the other two measures count changes in the number of businesses, which reflect both the business formation rate and the survival rate. The fourth measure emphasizes the income generated by entrepreneurs. States with entrepreneurs that generate higher income should be considered more entrepreneurial. The last measure examines a state's progress in technology businesses by looking at the number of patents per thousand residents.

These components imply that the entrepreneurship indicator is not simply a measure of state growth, but rather a measure of growth in the number of businesses, business earnings, and technological breakthroughs. As will be seen, some rapidly growing states in terms of overall population and economic activity such as Nevada, Arizona, and Florida have only above-average values for the entrepreneurship indicator, though some rapidly growing states such as Colorado and Idaho do have very high values. What this means is that a state such as Nebraska, which is a moderate-growth state, can score a high value for the index if entrepreneurship thrives in the state.

For each of the five measures, we calculated how much each state's performance differed from the performance of the median state. The state at the median received a value of 1.0. A state one standard deviation above the median received a value of 2.0 for that measure, while a state one standard deviation below the median received a value of 0.0 for that measure. A value for each state for each of the five measures was generated in this way.

A simple average of the five values for each state was then calculated. This was the value for the State Entrepreneurship Index. For example, in 2005, Nebraska had the values of 0.56, 1.27, 0.91, 0.96, and 0.54 for the five indicators. The aggregate index value was 0.85 – the average of these five numbers.

Table 3.7 reports the State Entrepreneurship Index values for 2004 and 2005, the two most recent years for which data is available. The index shows that the most entrepreneurial states are located in the West, Mountain, and Northeast regions.[1] The highest-ranked states typically had a strong value for nearly all measures, either above average or well above average.

In the Northeast, New York, New Jersey, Massachusetts, Connecticut, and Delaware were ranked high due to above-average values for business formation, but high values for the average income of proprietors. In the West and Mountain regions, Colorado, Idaho, and Oregon ranked high in business formation and patent activity. California was strong in both average income and patent activity, while Wyoming had strong rates of business formation.

Nebraska was ranked 34th in 2004 and 35th in 2005, and therefore was a below-average state in both years. The index value was below 1.0 in both periods. This finding is consistent with the results for the individual indicators presented earlier: Nebraska has been below average in most indicators of entrepreneurship in recent years. The state, however, is not far below average. Going forward, it will be important to track whether Nebraska is able to move above a value of 1.0 in the State Entrepreneurship Index. There is potential for improvement in business counts and business formation. There is also potential for improvement in the two other measures. As noted in the last chapter, strong growth in average proprietor income in the Omaha region since 1990 helped Nebraska improve its income per proprietor relative to the nation. This trend could re-emerge. There is also room for improvement in patent activity given that the state is home to two medical schools and a major research university.

Table 3.7: State Entrepreneurship Index, 2004–2005

State	2004 Rank	Index Value	State	2005 Rank	Index Value
Alabama	28	0.99	Alabama	36	0.80
Alaska	10	1.69	Alaska	43	0.56
Arizona	41	0.74	Arizona	26	1.11
Arkansas	45	0.71	Arkansas	41	0.67
California	8	1.77	California	6	1.74
Colorado	3	1.96	Colorado	2	2.17
Connecticut	9	1.72	Connecticut	4	1.87
Delaware	2	2.06	Delaware	10	1.53
Florida	16	1.37	Florida	14	1.36
Georgia	27	0.99	Georgia	33	0.90
Hawaii	50	0.16	Hawaii	39	0.75
Idaho	1	2.25	Idaho	1	2.44
Illinois	24	1.14	Illinois	15	1.35
Indiana	33	0.90	Indiana	40	0.74
Iowa	49	0.45	Iowa	49	0.46
Kansas	46	0.59	Kansas	31	0.92
Kentucky	43	0.72	Kentucky	45	0.53
Louisiana	32	0.93	Louisiana	44	0.54
Maine	23	1.16	Maine	50	0.32
Maryland	17	1.36	Maryland	12	1.42
Massachusetts	4	1.86	Massachusetts	5	1.84
Michigan	22	1.20	Michigan	22	1.24
Minnesota	31	0.94	Minnesota	16	1.32
Mississippi	36	0.87	Mississippi	48	0.47
Missouri	42	0.73	Missouri	38	0.77
Montana	26	1.06	Montana	46	0.53
Nebraska	**34**	**0.89**	**Nebraska**	**35**	**0.85**
Nevada	15	1.40	Nevada	29	1.03
New Hampshire	11	1.48	New Hampshire	13	1.37
New Jersey	5	1.83	New Jersey	3	2.08
New Mexico	47	0.55	New Mexico	25	1.11
New York	6	1.81	New York	7	1.74
North Carolina	38	0.83	North Carolina	37	0.77
North Dakota	37	0.84	North Dakota	32	0.90
Ohio	39	0.80	Ohio	34	0.90
Oklahoma	30	0.96	Oklahoma	20	1.25
Oregon	12	1.45	Oregon	11	1.49
Pennsylvania	19	1.31	Pennsylvania	17	1.31
Rhode Island	13	1.44	Rhode Island	8	1.58
South Carolina	48	0.49	South Carolina	27	1.11
South Dakota	44	0.72	South Dakota	42	0.63
Tennessee	21	1.28	Tennessee	28	1.04
Texas	20	1.29	Texas	21	1.25
Utah	18	1.35	Utah	18	1.29
Vermont	14	1.42	Vermont	19	1.29

Table 3.7: State Entrepreneurship Index, 2004–2005 (continued)

State	2004 Rank	Index Value	State	2005 Rank	Index Value
Virginia	29	0.97	Virginia	23	1.22
Washington	25	1.09	Washington	24	1.18
West Virginia	35	0.88	West Virginia	47	0.51
Wisconsin	40	0.78	Wisconsin	30	1.00
Wyoming	7	1.77	Wyoming	9	1.54

Source: Author's calculations.

ENTREPRENEURSHIP IN DISTRICTS

Nebraska overall had a below-average performance in entrepreneurship for the past few years. One key question is whether this was true statewide, or only in selected regions within the state. Table 3.8 displays employer establishment data for the six community college districts of Nebraska. It shows the counts of employer establishments each year from 2003 through 2006. All regions follow the statewide pattern of weak performance in 2003–2004 and rapid growth in 2004–2005. Growth last year, 2005–2006, was solid in most regions, except for the Western Community College district.

Table 3.8: Number of Employer Establishments, Community College Districts, 2003–2006

Community College District	Year				Average Annual Change in Counts		
	2003	2004	2005	2006ᵃ	2003–2004	2004–2005	2005–2006
Nebraska Totalᵇ	51,141	51,562	53,051	54,048	0.8%	2.9%	1.9%
Western CC	2,757	2,745	2,764	2,729	−0.4%	0.7%	−1.3%
Mid-Plains CC	2,902	2,889	2,932	2,952	−0.4%	1.5%	0.7%
Central CC	8,738	8,836	8,987	9,089	1.1%	1.7%	1.1%
Northeast CC	4,488	4,485	4,543	4,604	−0.1%	1.3%	1.3%
Metropolitan CC	18,384	18,501	19,052	19,416	0.6%	3.0%	1.9%
Southeast CC	11,585	11,710	12,017	12,266	1.1%	2.6%	2.1%

Notes:
[a]Estimate based on first three quarters of 2006.
[b]Districts do not sum to state totals since some establishments are classified as statewide rather than by a particular county in the state. The share not assigned to a particular county has risen over time.
Source: Bureau of Labor Statistics, Quarterly Census of Employment and Wages.

Establishment growth rates in the Metropolitan and Southeast Community College districts were roughly equal to the statewide average. This makes sense because the two regions contain the largest metropolitan areas of the state and account for three-fifths of the state's employer establishments. Growth rates in both regions, however, lagged national growth. Even the largest, most successful regions within Nebraska failed to match national averages for employer establishment growth.

Among other districts, the Central district was closest to matching the statewide average. Growth in employer establishments from 2003 through 2006 was much slower in the Northeast, Western, and Mid-Plains districts.

As is indicated in Table 3.9, there was growth in the number of employer establishments per person in each of the six districts. The strongest growth was in the Southeast, Central, and Northeast districts.

Table 3.9: Number of Employer Establishments per Person, Community College Districts, 2003–2006

Community College District	Per Capita Counts				Average Annual Change in Counts		
	2003	2004	2005	2006ᵃ	2003–2004	2004–2005	2005–2006
Nebraska Total	0.029	0.030	0.030	0.031	0.2%	2.2%	1.3%
Western CC	0.031	0.031	0.031	0.031	0.6%	1.3%	−0.5%
Mid-Plains CC	0.031	0.031	0.032	0.032	−0.5%	1.7%	1.2%
Central CC	0.029	0.029	0.030	0.030	0.9%	1.8%	0.9%
Northeast CC	0.028	0.029	0.029	0.030	0.6%	1.8%	2.0%
Metropolitan CC	0.028	0.028	0.028	0.028	−0.7%	1.5%	0.6%
Southeast CC	0.027	0.027	0.027	0.028	0.6%	1.9%	1.4%

Note: ᵃEstimate based on first three quarters of 2006.
Sources: Bureau of Labor Statistics, Quarterly Census of Employment and Wages; U.S. Census Bureau.

Table 3.10 reports growth in real (inflation-adjusted) income per proprietor in the six community college districts. In most districts, real income per proprietor grew from 2003–2004 and then declined from 2004–2005. In four of the districts, combined growth from 2003–2005 was positive. In other words, real income per proprietor was higher in 2005 than in 2003. In two other districts, the Western district and Metropolitan district, real income per proprietor declined in both years. These recent trends in the Metropolitan district are in sharp contrast to long-term trends, which showed real income per proprietor up sharply in the Metropolitan district from 1990 through 2005. In recent years, growing income in the Metropolitan district has not continued to drive state growth in income per proprietor.

Table 3.10: Income per Non-Farm Proprietor, Community College Districts, 2003–2005

Community College District	Year			Average Annual Change in Real Income	
	2003	2004	2005	2003–2004	2004–2005
Nebraska Total	$12,252	$12,443	$12,345	1.6%	−0.8%
Western CC	$9,274	$9,221	$8,924	−0.6%	−3.2%
Mid-Plains CC	$7,070	$7,385	$7,228	4.4%	−2.1%
Central CC	$7,396	$7,754	$7,644	4.8%	−1.4%
Northeast CC	$7,020	$7,461	$7,220	6.3%	−3.2%
Metropolitan CC	$21,164	$20,966	$20,871	−0.9%	−0.5%
Southeast CC	$8,747	$9,157	$9,126	4.7%	−0.3%

Sources: U.S. Bureau of Economic Analysis, Regional Economic Information System; U.S. Census Bureau.

CONCLUSION

Our analysis of entrepreneurship indicators over the past few years showed continued growth in the number of businesses and in business income. Growth rates in Nebraska, however, lagged the nation in new business starts, growth in employer establishments, and real income per non-farm proprietor. Nebraska also had a below-average value for the aggregate State Entrepreneurship Index. Our analysis of entrepreneurship in the community college districts indicated that slower establishment growth in the non-metropolitan districts accounted for slower growth in the number of employer establishments in Nebraska. The state's slow growth in real income per proprietor was due to a decline in the Metropolitan Community College district. This district has failed to drive income growth in the last few years, as it has since 1990. Overall, Nebraska is far from matching the level of entrepreneurial activity in the highest ranked states. Entrepreneurship index values should be tracked in the future to see if the state is able to improve to an above-average value among states and, ultimately, to achieve a high value.

NOTES

1. Our study examined other state rankings such as those of Beacon Hill institute (2006) and The Edward Lowe Foundation (2006). There was considerable overlap between the top entrepreneurial states identified in these studies and our State Entrepreneurship Index.

APPENDIX 3: State Entrepreneurship Index Components

Table 3.1a: Growth in the Number of Employer Establishments, 2003–2006

2003–2004			2004–2005			2005–2006		
State	Rank	Growth Rate	State	Rank	Growth Rate	State	Rank	Growth Rate
Nevada	1	8.8%	Arizona	1	7.0%	Arizona	1	9.4%
Delaware	2	8.3%	Florida	2	6.6%	S. Carolina	2	7.5%
Utah	3	6.4%	Utah	3	6.5%	Utah	3	7.5%
Florida	4	5.9%	Idaho	4	5.8%	Nevada	4	6.7%
Maine	5	5.8%	S. Carolina	5	5.8%	Idaho	5	5.8%
Massachusetts	6	3.2%	Nevada	6	5.5%	Oregon	6	5.7%
California	7	3.0%	Oregon	7	4.3%	Arkansas	7	5.0%
Maryland	8	3.0%	Minnesota	8	4.2%	Florida	8	4.9%
Alabama	9	2.9%	Colorado	9	4.0%	Kentucky	9	4.1%
Georgia	10	2.8%	Virginia	10	3.9%	Wyoming	10	3.9%
Wyoming	11	2.7%	Delaware	11	3.7%	New Mexico	11	3.8%
Alaska	12	2.7%	Wyoming	12	3.2%	California	12	3.8%
South Dakota	13	2.4%	Illinois	13	3.1%	Tennessee	13	3.5%
Virginia	14	2.3%	Louisiana	14	3.1%	Virginia	14	3.4%
Mississippi	15	2.2%	**Nebraska**	**15**	**2.9%**	Montana	15	3.4%
North Dakota	16	2.1%	Arkansas	16	2.8%	Illinois	16	3.3%
Arizona	17	2.0%	Georgia	17	2.8%	N. Carolina	17	3.3%
Texas	18	2.0%	Hawaii	18	2.7%	Minnesota	18	3.2%
Colorado	19	2.0%	Maryland	19	2.6%	Georgia	19	3.1%
Idaho	20	2.0%	Oklahoma	20	2.5%	Colorado	20	3.1%
N. Carolina	21	1.8%	North Dakota	21	2.5%	Hawaii	21	2.8%
New Hampshire	22	1.7%	New Jersey	22	2.5%	Kansas	22	2.6%
Rhode Island	23	1.7%	California	23	2.4%	New Jersey	23	2.4%
Iowa	24	1.6%	Wisconsin	24	2.4%	New Hampshire	24	2.3%
West Virginia	25	1.5%	South Dakota	25	2.3%	Texas	25	2.2%
Tennessee	26	1.5%	Alabama	26	2.3%	Oklahoma	26	2.1%
Vermont	27	1.5%	N. Carolina	27	2.2%	Louisiana	27	2.1%
Arkansas	28	1.4%	Alaska	28	2.1%	Maine	28	2.0%
Illinois	29	1.3%	Massachusetts	29	2.0%	South Dakota	29	2.0%
New York	30	1.3%	Texas	30	1.9%	**Nebraska**	**30**	**1.9%**
Missouri	31	1.3%	Kansas	31	1.9%	New York	31	1.8%
Michigan	32	1.2%	Mississippi	32	1.8%	Mississippi	32	1.7%
New Jersey	33	1.1%	Tennessee	33	1.8%	Missouri	33	1.6%
Oklahoma	34	1.0%	Rhode Island	34	1.7%	Washington	34	1.5%
Wisconsin	35	0.9%	New Mexico	35	1.6%	Maryland	35	1.5%
Nebraska	**36**	**0.8%**	New York	36	1.5%	Alaska	36	1.4%
Indiana	37	0.6%	Missouri	37	1.2%	Indiana	37	1.3%
Pennsylvania	38	0.6%	Pennsylvania	38	1.1%	Connecticut	38	1.2%
Connecticut	39	0.5%	Connecticut	39	1.1%	Iowa	39	1.1%

Table 3.1a: Growth in the Number of Employer Establishments, 2003–2006 (continued)

2003–2004			2004–2005			2005–2006		
State	Rank	Growth Rate	State	Rank	Growth Rate	State	Rank	Growth Rate
Louisiana	40	0.3%	Vermont	40	0.9%	Rhode Island	40	1.0%
Oregon	41	0.0%	Ohio	41	0.8%	North Dakota	41	0.9%
Kansas	42	−0.4%	Kentucky	42	0.7%	Vermont	42	0.7%
Kentucky	43	−0.4%	New Hampshire	43	0.7%	Michigan	43	0.6%
New Mexico	44	−0.6%	West Virginia	44	0.6%	Pennsylvania	44	0.5%
Minnesota	45	−0.7%	Michigan	45	0.4%	Ohio	45	0.4%
Montana	46	−0.7%	Indiana	46	0.4%	West Virginia	46	0.2%
Ohio	47	−1.7%	Iowa	47	0.3%	Wisconsin	47	0.1%
S. Carolina	48	−2.2%	Washington	48	−1.1%	Alabama	48	−0.4%
Hawaii	49	−5.1%	Maine	49	−2.6%	Delaware	49	−0.5%
Washington	50	−7.4%	Montana	50	−3.6%	Massachusetts	50	−4.5%

Source: Nebraska Workforce Development.

Table 3.2a: Firm Births per Person: For 50 U.S. States, 2003–2005

2003–2004			2004–2005		
State	Rank	Business Formation Rate	State	Rank	Business Formation Rate
Idaho	1	0.00571	Idaho	1	0.00668
Washington	2	0.00521	Colorado	2	0.00579
Colorado	3	0.00521	New Mexico	3	0.00560
Wyoming	4	0.00502	Wyoming	4	0.00521
Montana	5	0.00500	Montana	5	0.00515
Utah	6	0.00482	Washington	6	0.00489
Nevada	7	0.00468	Florida	7	0.00489
Florida	8	0.00458	Utah	8	0.00476
New Jersey	9	0.00416	New Jersey	9	0.00450
Delaware	10	0.00400	Nevada	10	0.00450
Maryland	11	0.00395	Oregon	11	0.00402
Oregon	12	0.00379	Delaware	12	0.00398
New Hampshire	13	0.00378	Maryland	13	0.00398
Vermont	14	0.00375	Arizona	14	0.00371
Rhode Island	15	0.00366	New Hampshire	15	0.00367
Georgia	16	0.00338	Rhode Island	16	0.00341
California	17	0.00330	California	17	0.00339
Maine	18	0.00329	Virginia	18	0.00335
Virginia	19	0.00327	Georgia	19	0.00334
New York	20	0.00327	Maine	20	0.00324

Table 3.2a: Firm Births per Person: For 50 U.S. States, 2003–2005 (continued)

2003–2004			2004–2005		
State	**Rank**	**Business Formation Rate**	**State**	**Rank**	**Business Formation Rate**
New Mexico	21	0.00303	New York	21	0.00322
Minnesota	22	0.00300	Pennsylvania	22	0.00310
Tennessee	23	0.00298	Vermont	23	0.00308
Hawaii	24	0.00297	Massachusetts	24	0.00306
Massachusetts	25	0.00292	North Carolina	25	0.00304
Arkansas	26	0.00288	Alaska	26	0.00302
Alaska	27	0.00285	Missouri	27	0.00300
South Carolina	28	0.00284	Hawaii	28	0.00299
Missouri	29	0.00283	North Dakota	29	0.00298
Nebraska	**30**	**0.00279**	Tennessee	30	0.00297
North Carolina	31	0.00278	South Carolina	31	0.00294
North Dakota	32	0.00276	**Nebraska**	**32**	**0.00293**
Pennsylvania	33	0.00269	Arkansas	33	0.00276
Oklahoma	34	0.00264	South Dakota	34	0.00273
Connecticut	35	0.00260	Connecticut	35	0.00264
Kansas	36	0.00247	Kansas	36	0.00259
Michigan	37	0.00245	Wisconsin	37	0.00248
Texas	38	0.00244	Texas	38	0.00248
Wisconsin	39	0.00239	Minnesota	39	0.00246
Illinois	40	0.00225	Oklahoma	40	0.00244
Indiana	41	0.00225	Michigan	41	0.00244
Arizona	42	0.00223	Illinois	42	0.00239
South Dakota	43	0.00221	Alabama	43	0.00234
Louisiana	44	0.00220	Indiana	44	0.00234
West Virginia	45	0.00218	Kentucky	45	0.00232
Kentucky	46	0.00214	Mississippi	46	0.00210
Mississippi	47	0.00214	Louisiana	47	0.00209
Alabama	48	0.00209	Iowa	48	0.00203
Iowa	49	0.00202	Ohio	49	0.00197
Nevada	50	0.00199	West Virginia	50	0.00193

Note: Firm births are measured between the months of March.
Sources: U.S. Small Business Administration; U.S. Census Bureau.

Table 3.3a: *Average Real (Inflation-Adjusted) Income of Non-Farm Proprietors, 2003–2005*

2003			2004			2005		
State	Rank	Real Income	State	Rank	Real Income	State	Rank	Real Income
New York	1	$22,091	Texas	1	$22,531	Texas	1	$22,675
Connecticut	2	$21,768	New York	2	$22,338	New York	2	$22,018
Texas	3	$21,012	Connecticut	3	$22,253	Connecticut	3	$21,948
New Jersey	4	$20,070	New Jersey	4	$20,612	New Jersey	4	$20,306
California	5	$17,154	Oklahoma	5	$19,751	Oklahoma	5	$19,714
Colorado	6	$16,996	Colorado	6	$18,522	Colorado	6	$18,367
Pennsylvania	7	$16,711	Pennsylvania	7	$17,366	Pennsylvania	7	$17,124
Tennessee	8	$16,655	Tennessee	8	$17,179	Tennessee	8	$17,083
Massachusetts	9	$16,553	Illinois	9	$17,103	California	9	$16,918
Oklahoma	10	$16,457	California	10	$17,062	Illinois	10	$16,671
Illinois	11	$16,407	Massachusetts	11	$16,952	Massachusetts	11	$16,501
Delaware	12	$15,411	Delaware	12	$16,286	Delaware	12	$16,266
Michigan	13	$14,313	Michigan	13	$15,475	Wyoming	13	$15,357
Rhode Island	14	$14,147	Wyoming	14	$15,183	Michigan	14	$15,075
Washington	15	$14,141	Louisiana	15	$14,850	Rhode Island	15	$14,335
Louisiana	16	$14,030	Rhode Island	16	$14,623	Washington	16	$14,141
Wyoming	17	$13,799	Washington	17	$14,619	Georgia	17	$13,979
New Hampshire	18	$13,584	Georgia	18	$14,047	Virginia	18	$13,859
Georgia	19	$13,455	Virginia	19	$13,844	Kansas	19	$13,699
Maryland	20	$13,321	New Hampshire	20	$13,798	New Hampshire	20	$13,616
Virginia	21	$13,238	Kansas	21	$13,726	Maryland	21	$13,448
Kansas	22	$12,842	Maryland	22	$13,450	Arizona	22	$13,070
Nevada	23	$12,557	Indiana	23	$13,105	Nevada	23	$13,012
Indiana	24	$12,534	Nevada	24	$12,673	Indiana	24	$12,862
Alaska	25	$12,509	Arizona	25	$12,665	Alabama	25	$12,490
Nebraska	26	$12,252	Ohio	26	$12,471	Alaska	26	$12,472
Arizona	27	$12,117	Alabama	27	$12,455	Nebraska	27	$12,345
Ohio	28	$12,078	Nebraska	28	$12,443	Ohio	28	$12,175
South Dakota	29	$11,936	Alaska	29	$12,391	Idaho	29	$12,114
Alabama	30	$11,855	West Virginia	30	$12,155	South Dakota	30	$12,085
Missouri	31	$11,851	South Dakota	31	$12,123	West Virginia	31	$12,052
Oregon	32	$11,742	Missouri	32	$11,973	Missouri	32	$11,880
West Virginia	33	$11,697	Idaho	33	$11,845	Utah	33	$11,861
Idaho	34	$11,427	Oregon	34	$11,814	Oregon	34	$11,853
Wisconsin	35	$11,350	Wisconsin	35	$11,629	Wisconsin	35	$11,436
Mississippi	36	$11,135	Utah	36	$11,599	New Mexico	36	$11,429
Kentucky	37	$11,094	Kentucky	37	$11,516	Kentucky	37	$11,378
Minnesota	38	$10,837	Mississippi	38	$11,419	North Dakota	38	$11,142
Arkansas	39	$10,682	New Mexico	39	$11,360	Arkansas	39	$11,110
New Mexico	40	$10,624	Arkansas	40	$11,177	Minnesota	40	$10,890
N. Carolina	41	$10,592	Minnesota	41	$11,113	S. Carolina	41	$10,869

Table 3.3a: Average Real (Inflation-Adjusted) Income of Non-Farm Proprietors, 2003–2005 (continued)

	2003			**2004**			**2005**	
		Real			**Real**			**Real**
State	**Rank**	**Income**	**State**	**Rank**	**Income**	**State**	**Rank**	**Income**
Utah	42	$10,528	S. Carolina	42	$10,926	N. Carolina	42	$10,815
North Dakota	43	$10,512	North Dakota	43	$10,919	Montana	43	$10,791
S. Carolina	44	$10,428	N. Carolina	44	$10,830	Florida	44	$10,501
Florida	45	$10,326	Montana	45	$10,648	Hawaii	45	$10,361
Montana	46	$9,984	Iowa	46	$10,375	Iowa	46	$10,300
Iowa	47	$9,951	Hawaii	47	$10,337	Mississippi	47	$9,947
Hawaii	48	$9,877	Florida	48	$10,066	Maine	48	$9,333
Maine	49	$9,169	Maine	49	$9,471	Vermont	49	$9,267
Vermont	50	$8,964	Vermont	50	$9,428	Louisiana	50	$6,983

Source: U.S. Department of Commerce, Bureau of Economic Analysis, Regional Economic Information System.

Table 3.4a: Number of Patents per Thousand Residents, 2003–2005

	2003			**2004**			**2005**	
		Patents per 1,000			**Patents per 1,000**			**Patents per 1,000**
State	**Rank**	**Persons**	**State**	**Rank**	**Persons**	**State**	**Rank**	**Persons**
Idaho	1	1.35290	Idaho	1	1.30654	Idaho	1	1.08370
Vermont	2	0.75168	Vermont	2	0.68944	Vermont	2	0.66036
Massachusetts	3	0.65082	Massachusetts	3	0.60659	California	3	0.54367
Minnesota	4	0.64439	California	4	0.60269	Massachusetts	4	0.51311
California	5	0.62242	Minnesota	5	0.58811	Oregon	5	0.50812
New Hampshire	6	0.56769	Oregon	6	0.54804	Minnesota	6	0.50363
Connecticut	7	0.52953	New Hampshire	7	0.52467	Connecticut	7	0.47905
Oregon	8	0.52427	Colorado	8	0.49777	Colorado	8	0.42288
Colorado	9	0.50616	Connecticut	9	0.49286	New Hampshire	9	0.41169
Delaware	10	0.45540	Delaware	10	0.48989	Delaware	10	0.40511
New Jersey	11	0.45410	Michigan	11	0.40839	Washington	11	0.39448
Michigan	12	0.41894	Washington	12	0.39352	Michigan	12	0.36274
Washington	13	0.41042	New Jersey	13	0.38636	New Jersey	13	0.32954
Wisconsin	14	0.38084	Wisconsin	14	0.35917	Wisconsin	14	0.31768
New York	15	0.35975	New York	15	0.34305	Rhode Island	15	0.29062
Ohio	16	0.34027	Rhode Island	16	0.34108	New York	16	0.27465
Illinois	17	0.31337	Utah	17	0.32377	Arizona	17	0.26844
Utah	18	0.30733	Arizona	18	0.30110	Utah	18	0.25860

Table 3.4a: Number of Patents per Thousand Residents, 2003–2005 (continued)

2003			2004			2005		
State	Rank	Patents per 1,000 Persons	State	Rank	Patents per 1,000 Persons	State	Rank	Patents per 1,000 Persons
Arizona	19	0.30704	Ohio	19	0.29813	Illinois	19	0.25828
Rhode Island	20	0.30239	Illinois	20	0.29528	Texas	20	0.24092
Texas	21	0.28806	Texas	21	0.27707	Ohio	21	0.23774
Pennsylvania	22	0.28782	Pennsylvania	22	0.26039	Maryland	22	0.22953
Maryland	23	0.28638	Maryland	23	0.25859	Iowa	23	0.21210
Indiana	24	0.27068	Iowa	24	0.24918	N. Carolina	24	0.21205
N. Carolina	25	0.25833	N. Carolina	25	0.24323	Pennsylvania	25	0.20523
Iowa	26	0.24167	Indiana	26	0.23862	Indiana	26	0.19885
New Mexico	27	0.21517	Nevada	27	0.20407	Nevada	27	0.18364
Nevada	28	0.20302	New Mexico	28	0.20151	Kansas	28	0.16556
Florida	29	0.18367	Kansas	29	0.19720	Florida	29	0.15235
Kansas	30	0.18005	Florida	30	0.17211	Georgia	30	0.14870
Georgia	31	0.17542	Georgia	31	0.16698	New Mexico	31	0.14123
Virginia	32	0.16934	Virginia	32	0.15805	Virginia	32	0.13577
Wyoming	33	0.16750	Missouri	33	0.15557	North Dakota	33	0.12764
Tennessee	34	0.16677	Tennessee	34	0.14850	Montana	34	0.12731
Missouri	35	0.16543	Montana	35	0.14142	S. Carolina	35	0.12692
Oklahoma	36	0.16066	Oklahoma	36	0.13909	Missouri	36	0.12626
S. Carolina	37	0.15667	S. Carolina	37	0.13851	Oklahoma	37	0.12107
Nebraska	**38**	**0.13817**	**Nebraska**	**38**	**0.13108**	Maine	38	0.12062
Montana	39	0.13629	South Dakota	39	0.11426	Tennessee	39	0.11955
Maine	40	0.12623	Kentucky	40	0.11182	**Nebraska**	**40**	**0.11660**
Kentucky	41	0.12006	Wyoming	41	0.10880	Wyoming	41	0.10810
South Dakota	42	0.11651	Maine	42	0.10503	Kentucky	42	0.09035
Alabama	43	0.10211	North Dakota	43	0.10380	South Dakota	43	0.08776
North Dakota	44	0.09801	Alabama	44	0.09120	Alabama	44	0.07893
Louisiana	45	0.09775	Louisiana	45	0.08608	Louisiana	45	0.06611
West Virginia	46	0.07796	Alaska	46	0.07460	Arkansas	46	0.05512
Hawaii	47	0.07707	Hawaii	47	0.06829	Alaska	47	0.05428
Alaska	48	0.06638	West Virginia	48	0.06130	West Virginia	48	0.05402
Arkansas	49	0.06462	Arkansas	49	0.05825	Hawaii	49	0.04555
Mississippi	50	0.06402	Mississippi	50	0.05497	Mississippi	50	0.04367

Source: Statistical Abstract of the United States, "Patents by State."

Table 3.5a: Growth in the Number of Non-Farm Proprietors, per Capita, 2003–2005

	2003–2004			2004–2005	
State	**Rank**	**Growth in Non-Farm Proprietors per Capita**	**State**	**Rank**	**Growth in Non-Farm Proprietors per Capita**
Alaska	1	10.1%	Rhode Island	1	6.0%
Wyoming	2	6.2%	Massachusetts	2	5.7%
West Virginia	3	6.2%	Connecticut	3	5.4%
Mississippi	4	6.1%	New Jersey	4	5.4%
Kentucky	5	6.1%	Ohio	5	5.3%
Alabama	6	6.0%	Michigan	6	5.3%
Ohio	7	5.9%	New York	7	5.1%
Louisiana	8	5.8%	Pennsylvania	8	5.0%
Oregon	9	5.8%	Maryland	9	5.0%
Massachusetts	10	5.8%	New Hampshire	10	5.0%
Pennsylvania	11	5.6%	Vermont	11	5.0%
New York	12	5.4%	Illinois	12	4.8%
Tennessee	13	5.3%	Louisiana	13	4.8%
Indiana	14	5.2%	California	14	4.7%
Nebraska	**15**	**5.2%**	West Virginia	15	4.7%
Connecticut	16	5.2%	Alabama	16	4.7%
Maine	17	5.2%	North Dakota	17	4.7%
Rhode Island	18	5.1%	Indiana	18	4.6%
North Dakota	19	5.0%	Wisconsin	19	4.6%
Vermont	20	4.9%	Maine	20	4.5%
Washington	21	4.9%	Minnesota	21	4.5%
New Jersey	22	4.8%	Kansas	22	4.5%
Montana	23	4.8%	Oklahoma	23	4.5%
Michigan	24	4.7%	Hawaii	24	4.5%
California	25	4.7%	Virginia	25	4.4%
Illinois	26	4.6%	Mississippi	26	4.4%
Maryland	27	4.5%	Missouri	27	4.4%
South Carolina	28	4.5%	Kentucky	28	4.4%
Arkansas	29	4.5%	Wyoming	29	4.4%
New Hampshire	30	4.4%	South Carolina	30	4.3%
South Dakota	31	4.2%	Iowa	31	4.3%
North Carolina	32	4.2%	Colorado	32	4.2%
Hawaii	33	4.1%	Tennessee	33	4.1%
Florida	34	4.1%	**Nebraska**	**34**	**4.1%**
Delaware	35	4.0%	Arkansas	35	4.0%
Colorado	36	3.9%	Montana	36	4.0%
Wisconsin	37	3.9%	Washington	37	3.9%
Missouri	38	3.8%	North Carolina	38	3.9%
Minnesota	39	3.7%	New Mexico	39	3.8%

Table 3.5a: Growth in the Number of Non-Farm Proprietors, per Capita, 2003–2005 (continued)

2003–2004			2004–2005		
State	**Rank**	**Growth in Non-Farm Proprietors per Capita**	**State**	**Rank**	**Growth in Non-Farm Proprietors per Capita**
Virginia	40	3.6%	Oregon	40	3.8%
Kansas	41	3.2%	South Dakota	41	3.7%
New Mexico	42	3.2%	Delaware	42	3.6%
Georgia	43	3.2%	Florida	43	3.5%
Arizona	44	3.1%	Georgia	44	3.5%
Idaho	45	2.9%	Texas	45	3.4%
Iowa	46	2.9%	Alaska	46	3.4%
Texas	47	2.8%	Idaho	47	2.6%
Oklahoma	48	2.7%	Utah	48	2.6%
Utah	49	1.8%	Nevada	49	2.1%
Nevada	50	1.4%	Arizona	50	2.1%

Sources: U.S. Small Business Administration; U.S. Census Bureau.

CHAPTER 4

Attitudes Toward Entrepreneurship

An increase in entrepreneurial activity holds great promise for creating many opportunities for business expansion, economic development, and social welfare in Nebraska. For this promise and these opportunities to be realized, the climate for entrepreneurship in Nebraska needs to be investigated. It is this climate that can significantly influence whether entrepreneurs, current or potential, are willing to assume the risk of starting a business, or remain in the state or community once the business is successful. The two previous chapters studied this issue by presenting data on economic and business conditions. This chapter shifts the focus and measures the entrepreneurial climate using survey data collected by Gallup on opinions and attitudes on entrepreneurship and business among Nebraskans.[1]

The survey analysis was conducted in two ways, both of which complemented each other. The first approach was to find out what the general public in Nebraska, those persons who are 18 years of age or older, thought about entrepreneurship and related business issues. Such a survey analysis provided insights about the interest in starting new businesses in the state and the support for activities that contribute to entrepreneurship and community development. For this purpose, survey data were collected from 2,460 individuals in 2005 and another 2,475 individuals in 2006.[2]

The second approach was to find out how owners of small businesses in Nebraska viewed entrepreneurship and business in the state. This analysis, similar to the one for the general public, was equally important because it revealed what small business owners thought about the opportunities for entrepreneurship in the state and how entrepreneurship can be encouraged and expanded. This group is especially important to survey because these owners often are the ones with the most recent experience with new enterprises. Most new businesses start with few employees, and may remain limited in size for many years until economic and business conditions change. For this purpose, data were collected in 2005 from 555 owners of Nebraska small businesses that had 100 or fewer employees and in 2006 from another 567 small business owners with the same characteristics.[3]

The climate for entrepreneurship in Nebraska is affected by many factors, so surveying opinions and attitudes to measure it covers a broad range of topics. Entrepreneurial attitudes can be directly reflected by interest in starting a business, reasons to be or not to be an entrepreneur, and challenges to entrepreneurship. Prior education and training in schools or colleges and universities affect people's knowledge of business, and thus most likely their degree of confidence and willingness to undertake the new-venture challenge. Opinions on various economic and business topics, such as markets, taxes, regulation, finance, economic development, and business succession, provide additional indicators of the climate for entrepreneurship.

The survey findings are too lengthy to be reported in one chapter because of the many topics. To give the results more emphasis and clarity, they are organized across several chapters. The current chapter assesses attitudes toward entrepreneurship using questions that are sorted into two sections. The first section reports on interest in starting a business and analyzes the age factor in this decision. The second section discusses the reasons why people do and do not start a business. Chapter 5 continues the survey analysis by offering insights on knowledge and education about entrepreneurship and business. In Chapter 6 the survey investigation turns to opinions on the role of government, and views of business, and issues that can affect business and economic development.

One final point should be noted before the presentation of the survey results and associated tables in this chapter and the next two chapters. Some questions on the 2005 and 2006 surveys were the same and others were different. About a third of the survey questions were asked only in 2005, so the sample size for those questions is 2,460 for the general public and 555 for small business owners. Another third of the questions were asked only in 2006, so those questions have a sample size of 2,475 for the general public and 567 for small business owners. A final third of the questions were asked both years. For these questions, the two samples were combined, so the sample size was 4,935 for the general public and 1,122 for business owners.[4]

INTEREST IN ENTREPRENEURSHIP IN NEBRASKA

Interest in entrepreneurship is strong among the general public in Nebraska as indicated by their responses to the question of whether they wanted to start a business of their own (Table 4.1). Almost one third (32%) of the general public stated they would like to start their own business. About another one in ten (11%) stated that they have already started a business. The combined percentages indicate that more than four in ten (43%) of the general public hold entrepreneurial aspirations or have acted on them. This percentage is impressive given that many in the general public are not in a position to act on their entrepreneurial aspirations because they are retired or have other commitments that restrict this choice.

Table 4.1: Want to Start Own Business[a]

Response	General Public (n=4,935)	Age 18–29 (850)	Age 30–39 (857)	Age 40–49 (955)	Age 50+ (2,140)
	%	%	%	%	%
Yes	32	55	45	37	15
Already have own business	11	5	13	14	11
Total of those interested in entrepreneurship	**43**	**60**	**58**	**51**	**26**
No	56	38	42	48	73
Don't know/Refused	1	2	0	1	1

Note: [a]"Do you think you would want to start a business of your own?" [3][5]

The effect of age on entrepreneurial aspirations clearly shows when the results are subdivided by age ranges. Among those aged 18–29 in Nebraska, over five in ten (55%) wanted to start a business and another five percent already had started a business. This strong interest in entrepreneurship among six in ten (60%) of the youngest adults in Nebraska suggests that programs, instruction, and activities for advancing entrepreneurship among this age group would find a very receptive audience.

The same conclusion applies to the other adult age groups until age 50. Among 30–39 year-olds, more than four in ten (45%) were interested in entrepreneurship. Although this interest declines by ten percentage points from the 18–29 group, it is partially offset by a rise in the percentage who had already started a business (from 5% to 13%). The total percentage (58%) still shows that almost six in ten of this group were interested in or committed to entrepreneurship, which is almost the same total as in the 18–29 age group.

A similar result is found with the 40–49 year-old group. Compared with those 30–39 years old, a slightly smaller percentage among those aged 40–49 were interested in starting a business (37%), but a slightly larger percentage had already started a business (14%). The total percentage (51%) shows that more than half in this group were interested in entrepreneurship.

It is only when Nebraskans reach 50 years of age or older that interest in entrepreneurship wanes to a significant degree and falls to a low level (26% total). This drop is to be expected because many Nebraskans among this group were employed, were nearing retirement, or had already retired.

This interest in entrepreneurship is not a passing thought (Table 4.2). More than four in ten (44%) of the general public in Nebraska who said they wanted to start a business also said they are either *very likely* (25%) or *likely* (19%) to act on the idea. By contrast, over five in ten (55%) stated they were *undecided* (29%), *unlikely* (15%), or *not at all likely* (11%) to start a business.

Table 4.2: Likely to Act on Idea to Start Own Business[a]

	General Public (n=1,225)[b]	Age			
		18–29	30–39	40–49	50+
Response		(217)	(272)	(318)	(403)
	%	%	%	%	%
5 Very likely	25	30	23	22	23
4	19	21	21	18	16
3	29	30	27	34	24
2	15	12	18	17	14
1 Not at all likely	11	7	10	10	22

Notes:
[a]"Using a five-point scale, where 5 is very likely, and 1 is not at all likely, how likely are you to act on this idea to start your own business?" [3]
[b]For YES respondents on whether you'd want to start a business of your own (see Table 4.1).

Age again influences the response of the general public who said they wanted to start a business. Five in ten (51%) of those aged 18–29 stated they were either likely or very likely to act on the idea of starting a business. The percentage falls slightly among those aged 30–39 (to 44%). It falls slightly again with the 40–49 age group (to 40%). At 50 years of age or more, about the same percentage (39%) also stated they are very likely or likely to pursue their entrepreneurial interests as those in the 40–49 age range. What these results suggest is that although interest in entrepreneurship and the likeliness of acting on that interest may decline with age, among those interested in and likely to pursue entrepreneurship, the entrepreneurial spirit is alive in many Nebraskans regardless of age.

To gain a further perspective on how important age is for starting a business, small business owners in Nebraska were asked about the age when they first thought about starting or owning their own businesses (Table 4.3). What should not be surprising is that these first thoughts of entrepreneurship came to many at a relatively young age. Almost two-thirds (64%) first thought about starting a business when they were under 30 years of age. Another two in ten (20%) business owners said that they first thought about starting a business during their thirties.

Table 4.3: Age When Thought of Starting Own Business[a]

Response	Business Owners (n=1,122)
Younger than 18 years old	14%
18–29 years old	50
30–39	20
40–49	9
Over 50 years old	5
Don't know/Refused	3

Note: [a]"How old were you when you first thought about starting or owning your own business?" [3]

What these results indicate is that the first thought about entrepreneurship occurred for the great majority (84%) of Nebraska small business owners when they were younger than 40 years old. Some Nebraska small business owners, of course, consider entrepreneurship when they are 40 years of age or older and after they've had more life or business experience, but this view is more likely to be the exception and not the norm for initial thinking about entrepreneurship. The entrepreneurial imagination starts early in the lives of most eventual entrepreneurs. These findings suggest that programs or education for entrepreneurship need to begin at an early age because these years are an especially formative period in shaping the thinking of potential, future entrepreneurs.

Time is a factor affecting entrepreneurship along with age. A follow-up question in 2006 was asked of 2,475 members of the general public who stated they were likely to start a business to find out how soon that would be. More than half the group (56%) had a relatively short perspective on becoming an entrepreneur (15% said it would be in a year or less; 22% stated it would be in 2–4 years; and 19% replied it would be in five years). The rest of the group (43%) had a longer time horizon on entrepreneurship (8% said it would be in 6–10 years and 35% said it would be in more than ten years).

Several questions were included on the survey to assess the general support for entrepreneurship. Starting a business is a laudable career in the view of the Nebraska general public and small business owners. Among those in the general public who have children, nine in ten (91%) said they wanted their child to become an entrepreneur (Table 4.4). This highly positive view may be due to the opportunities entrepreneurship can offer a person either in terms of income or control over their lives.

Table 4.4: Child Become an Entrepreneur[a]

Response	General Public (n=1,018)	Business Owners (n=555)
	%	%
Yes	91	81
No	6	13
Don't know/Refused	3	6

Note: [a]"Would you want your child to become an entrepreneur?" [1]

Business owners were somewhat less enthusiastic than the general public when asked this question, but eight in ten (81%) business owners wanted their child to become an entrepreneur. A likely reason for this difference in views is that business owners probably understand fully what such a career path requires and were less idealistic in their thinking than the general public. A few small business owners may have thought the demands, risks, or sacrifices involved in starting and running a business were not a suitable career path for their children. Nevertheless, entrepreneurship is a career path that the great majority of both the general public and business owners in Nebraska would recommend to their children.

Further probing on this matter was conducted just with business owners. The question gave these owners the choice of either starting a business of their own or working for someone else who owns a business to see their preferences for entrepreneurship over being an employee (Table 4.5). As was the case with the child question, the response was overwhelmingly supportive of entrepreneurship. More than three-fourths (77%) of these business owners would rather start their own businesses than work for someone else. The response, however, was not unanimous for similar reasons cited with the previous question. Being a business owner typically requires a great deal of work and demands a wide of set of business skills for being successful. Not all business owners may want to work such long hours or think they have the necessary skills for running a successful business, and thus may prefer to work for someone else (29%) if they had the chance to start over.

Table 4.5: Start Own Business or Work for Someone Else[a]

Response	Business Owners (n=567)
Starting own business	77%
Working for someone else	29
Don't know/Refused/Other	5

Note: [a]"If you had a choice between: (1) starting your own business, or (2) working for someone else who owns a business, which would you rather do?" [2]

Entrepreneurs typically do not just start one business (Table 4.6). In fact, only a third (33%) said that this business was the only business they had either started or owned. Two-thirds (67%) of small business owners stated that they had started at least one *other* business (29% said they had started one other business, 22% said they had started two other businesses, and 16% said they had started three or more other businesses). These responses show the real passion for entrepreneurship among Nebraska business owners. Most of them are willing to launch a business venture more than once during their business careers, indicating that entrepreneurship is not a one-time event and often leads to multiple start-ups for the Nebraska economy.

Table 4.6: Number of Other Businesses Started[a]

Response	Business Owners (n=555)
None other than this one	33%
1	29
2	22
3 or more	16

Note: [a]"In addition to this business, how many businesses have you ever started or owned?" [1]

In this respect, age also may have an important influence on the number of business starts because the younger a person is when he or she starts the first business, the longer lifetime the person has to start other businesses. Once a person starts one business, that business owner is highly likely to start other businesses during a lifetime. The fact that there is serial entrepreneurship is another good reason to encourage more entrepreneurship in Nebraska at an early age. From a state perspective, there will be a multiplier effect to the Nebraska economy from someone becoming a serial entrepreneur that makes a substantial contribution to all the positive outcomes from entrepreneurship: economic growth, jobs creation, higher wage and salary incomes, wealth creation, more philanthropy, and greater community development.

REASONS AND CHALLENGES

Although the general public in Nebraska typically evaluates small business from a consumer perspective, they show a good understanding of the entrepreneurial perspective when given a list of reasons to consider for why *other* people want to start a business (Table 4.7). Nine in ten (91%) of the general public either *strongly agreed* (70%) or *agreed* (21%) that the reason people go into business was to be their own boss, with most of them offering the *strongly agree* response. More than eight in ten (86%) of the general public either strongly agreed (57%) or agreed (29%) that the reason people often become entrepreneurs was to build something for the family, but there was clearly less strong agreement with this family option than was the case with the boss option. Use of skills and abilities as the motivating reason drew a similar percentage agreement (84%) as that of building something for the family and had a similar split between strongly agree (51%) and agree (33%).

Table 4.7: Reasons People Go into Business[a]

Reasons	SA	A	U	D	SD
	%	%	%	%	%
A. To be their own boss					
General public (n=4,935)	70	21	6	2	2
Business owners (n=567)	72	16	10	1	1
B. To build something for their family					
General public	57	29	12	3	2
Business owners	62	25	10	2	1
C. To use their skills and abilities					
General public	51	33	13	2	2
Business owners	58	28	13	1	0
D. To earn lots of money					
General public	34	26	30	7	4
Business owners	30	22	35	6	7
E. To overcome a challenge					
General public	20	24	35	13	7
Business owners	21	29	30	13	8

Note: [a]"Using a five-point scale, where '5' means you strongly agree (SA), and '1' means that you strongly disagree (SD), do you think people go into business:" [3P, 2B]

Of less importance as a motivating reason for entrepreneurship for the general public was the desire to earn lots of money (60%) with just over a third strongly agreeing (34%) and just over a quarter agreeing (26%) with that statement. Most of the general public do not see the reason for entrepreneurship as having something to do with overcoming a challenge (44%). The responses to the monetary option, however, are important because they reveal sophistication in the thinking about entrepreneurship. Most Nebraskans understand that the reasons for starting a business are not about making money and becoming rich for most entrepreneurs. They recognize that there are other more important psychological or personal factors driving individuals to start businesses and make them successful.

Owners of small businesses in Nebraska hold about the same views and in the same proportions as the general public in Nebraska regarding reasons for why *other* people want to start a business. Almost nine in ten (88%) of small business owners either strongly agreed (72%) or agreed (16%) that the reason people go into business was to be their own boss, with most of them offering the *strongly agree* response, as was the case with the general public. Next in order of importance was building something for the family (87% agreement). Compared with being your own boss, however, slightly less (62% versus 72%) strongly agreed and slightly more (25% versus 16%) agreed with this reason. Using skills and abilities was also high on the list in terms of agreement (86%), but slightly less strongly agree (58%) and slightly more agreed (28%) than was the case with the two higher ranked options.

What also is remarkable is that both the general public and small business owners in Nebraska hold about the same opinion of the less important reasons other people start businesses. Just over half (52%) of small business owners show agreement that the motivating reason for entrepreneurship is the desire to earn lots of money, but only three in ten strongly agreed (30%) and just more than two in ten (22%) agreed. Half (50%) of small business owners do not attribute entrepreneurship as having something to do with overcoming a challenge, with strong agreement from about two in ten (21%) and agreement from less than three in ten (29%). As was the case with the general public, small business owners understand that most entrepreneurs are not driven by monetary reasons, but rather by the desire to take control of their lives and be independent, to build something for the family, or to use skills and abilities. These deep-seated psychological and personal reasons for starting a business have a great deal of power and influence over entrepreneurial behavior.

Further evidence of this understanding comes from an open-ended question that was asked of both the general public and business owners in Nebraska (Table 4.8). In this case, the respondents were *not* asked to interpret the reasons that motivated *other* people start businesses, but instead were asked the reasons from their personal perspectives. Consequently, the general public sample was restricted to just those members who also stated that they were interested in starting their own businesses (see Table 4.1). The major reason for starting a new business, given by over half (51%) of those in the general public who were interested in doing so, was the independence factor – being your own boss. Earning lots of money as a motivating reason was cited significantly less often. Less than two in ten (18%) of the general public supplied this answer as their reason for becoming an entrepreneur. The only other answer drawing more than a one in ten response was to use my skills and abilities (13%).

Table 4.8: Major Reason for Wanting to Start Business[a]

Response	General Public (n=1,021)[b]	Business Owners (n=555)
	%	%
To be my own boss	51	63
To build something for the family	7	13
To use my skills and abilities	13	8
To help the community/provide jobs	6	7
To earn lots of money	18	6
To overcome a challenge	5	3
Other	1	–
Don't know/Refused	–	1

Notes:
[a]For the General Public, the question was: "What is the major reason you might want to start a business of your own?" For Business Owners, the question was: "What is the major reason why you wanted to start and/or own a business?" [1]
[b]Those responding "Yes" to wanting to start own business plus those already owning a business (see Table 4.1).

Small business owners in Nebraska were asked the question of why they wanted to start or own their current businesses. The overwhelming response, given by over six in ten (63%) of these business owners, was to be in charge of their lives by being their own boss. The other major reasons stated were to build something for the family (13%), use skills and abilities (8%), and help the community and provide jobs (7%). The combination of these four reasons accounted for more than nine in ten (91%) of all the open-ended responses. Earning a lot of money was not a major motivating reason for business owners. It was cited by only about one in 20 (6%) business owners and was about as important as overcoming a challenge (3%).

One of the major reasons why small business owners wanted to start a business was typically job or work related (Table 4.9). When the small business owners were asked in an open-ended question about the first significant event or experience that prompted them to start or own their current businesses, over a third of them (38%) cited a job-related reason such as the need for independence (16%), a past job or experience (9%), job dissatisfaction or burnout (8%), losing a job or becoming unemployed (4%), or needing money (1%). Clearly, the desire for making your own job and being your own boss instead of taking a job offered by someone else or accepting the insecurity of employment in the job market was a major motivating reason for why small business owners in Nebraska wanted to be entrepreneurs. Most of these individuals become entrepreneurs because of this desire for control or independence or because they saw an opportunity.

Table 4.9: Event or Experience Prompting Business Start[a]

Response	Business Owners (n=555)	
	%	%
Economic Freedom/Job-Related Issues		38
1. Need for independence/own boss	16	
2. Past job or job experience	9	
3. Dissatisfaction with job/job burnout	8	
4. Losing a job or becoming unemployed	4	
5. Needed money	1	
Economic Opportunity/Conditions		32
1. Spotted a viable idea or opportunity	27	
2. Market/Demand conditions were right	5	
Other Experiences		24
1. Events or experience in family	20	
2. Courses of educational experiences	3	
3. Hobbies	1	
Other		–
Don't know/Refused		5

Note: [a]"In retrospect, what was the first significant event or experience that prompted you to start or own this business?" [1]

Other events or experiences that stimulate entrepreneurship may be more positive and associated with risk taking. Some business owners thought the economic condition or opportunity was right (32%), because they either had a creative idea (27%), or thought the market would like the good or service (5%). Still other small business owners in Nebraska cited unspecified experiences (24%) such as ones involving the family (20%), an educational experience (3%), or a hobby (1%).

Small business owners in Nebraska identified many challenges to starting a business, but some of the challenges were thought to be more difficult than initially anticipated for people who start a business (Table 4.10). These responses are discussed in ascending order. About half (46%) of small business owners thought that coming up with good ideas was more difficult. About six in ten thought that either competing with other businesses (61%) or obtaining loans and financing (62%) were more difficult. About seven in ten noted that it was developing sales (69%). About eight in ten thought the unanticipated challenge was controlling costs for the business (78%) or they identified the problem of handling government regulation and red tape (79%) as an unexpected challenge. This last challenge is an external factor that catches most entrepreneurs by surprise because they are focused on developing a product and delivering it to the market in the least costly way when they start a business, and they are not aware of the extent to which government can influence how a small business operates.

Table 4.10: More Difficult Challenges in Starting a Business[a]

Challenges	General Public (n=2,460)	Business Owners (n=555)
	%	%
Handling government regulation and red tape	77	79
Controlling costs	84	78
Developing sales	81	69
Obtaining loans and financing	75	62
Competing with other businesses	81	61
Coming up with good ideas	64	46

Note: [a]"Which of the following challenges do you think prove to be more difficult than initially anticipated by people who start a new business?" [1]

The general public's view of the challenges that were more difficult for small business than initially anticipated differed substantially from those of small business owners. In almost every case, the general public rated an option as being more challenging than anticipated than small business owners rated the option. The explanation for the difference is attributable to the limited understanding among the general public about how small businesses are started and also how they work.

Three-fourths (75%) of the general public thought obtaining loans and financing was a more difficult challenge than expected, but the percentage who thought so was much higher than the percentage of business owners (62%) who selected this option. Similarly, competing with other businesses was viewed as a more difficult challenge than expected by the general public (81%) than was the case among business owners (61%). Controlling costs was viewed as more difficult by the general public than business owners (84% versus 78%), as was developing sales (81% versus 69%).

The one item on which both the general public and small business owners in Nebraska showed the most agreement was the difficulties created for new businesses by government regulation and red tape. Almost eight in ten (77% or 79%) in both groups thought this option was more challenging than initially anticipated by people who start new businesses.

What is evident from further surveying of small business owners in Nebraska is that the challenges or obstacles to starting a business are many and varied, when the need for financial support to start the business is omitted from this open-ended question (Table 4.11). Small business owners in Nebraska cited many obstacles, but they can be categorized into four types: management concerns (45%), handling the risk (16%), poor economic conditions (14%), and lack of education (13%).

Table 4.11: Greatest Non-Financial Obstacle[a]

Response	Business Owners (n=555)	
	%	%
A. Management Factors		**45**
Developing clientele	16	
Being able to handle gov. regulations	13	
Concerns about managing and motivating people	10	
Coming up with a good idea or opportunity	6	
B. Risk – Being able to handle it		**16**
C. Economic Conditions		**14**
Poor economic conditions	6	
Location	5	
Competition	3	
D. Education Factors		**13**
Young age or lack of experience	5	
Lack of education and skills	5	
Lack of personal knowledge about technology	3	
Other		**4**
None		**1**
Don't know/Refused		**7**

Note: [a]"Other than financing, what do you think was your greatest obstacle to starting your current business?" [1]

What is included in the largest type, management, deserves more elaboration because it reveals more about the thinking of entrepreneurs. Near the top of the list of obstacles in this category is being able to handle government regulation and red tape, which was also cited in the previous question on challenges. Many small business owners in Nebraska viewed government as more of a hindrance than an aid to starting a business. The other list of management obstacles are to be expected and have more to do with growing the business, such as developing the clientele (16%), being able to manage and motivate people (10%), and coming up with a good idea (6%).

Among the education factors cited as obstacles were young age or lack of experience (5%), a lack of education and skills (5%), and a lack of knowledge about technology (3%). These cited factors, and even the ones related to management, risk, or economic conditions, all suggest that educational programs to prepare people for entrepreneurship serve an important purpose in helping potential entrepreneurs in overcoming obstacles to starting a business. Education may not solve all these perceived problems, but it can prepare potential entrepreneurs for the types of problems they are likely to encounter and can help them develop skills to manage a business. To the extent that entrepreneurship is a career more attractive to younger adults, such education can help young entrepreneurs compensate for their youth or lack of experience.

The above discussion of obstacles is suggestive of reasons why people might not start a business, but it is important to seek such reasons with more direct questioning and obtain responses from both business owners and the general public. Not everyone wants to become an entrepreneur and it can be instructive to find out why because such obstacles or problems perhaps could be addressed or ameliorated to encourage more people to start businesses.

Two questions on the survey provide insights on people's perceptions of reasons for not starting a business. The first one was close ended and gave suggested reasons for why other people might not start a business (Table 4.12). The list of such factors or roadblocks to entrepreneurship included the appetite for risk, the time demand, the education required, the need for money to start the business, and the difficulty of managing people. The question was asked of both the general public and business owners to get the contrasting perspective.

The responses that received the most agreement from business owners are ordered from A to E because they probably have the most insight for evaluating this question. What comes to the top of the list is the propensity for accepting risk (82% strongly agree or agree). Entrepreneurship is by its nature a risk-taking endeavor and if people do not have much tolerance for accepting risk, they are unlikely to become entrepreneurs. Next in order of importance as a barrier to entrepreneurship is that it requires too much money to get the business started (74% agreement). The difficulty of managing and motivating people also is an issue, with over half (57%) citing that problem. About the same percentage (54% agreement) also stated that the time demands required for starting a business prevented many people from starting one. At the bottom of the list for business owners is the amount of education. Few business owners in Nebraska think that a major reason people do not start businesses is because it requires lots of education.

Table 4.12: Reasons People Do Not Start a Business[a]

Reasons	SA	A	U	D	SD
	%	%	%	%	%
A. It is too risky					
General public (n=2,475)	46	28	16	5	4
Business owners (n=567)	53	29	10	5	3
B. It requires too much money					
General public	49	26	16	5	4
Business owners	48	26	17	6	3
C. It is difficult to manage people					
General public	19	22	34	14	9
Business owners	31	26	28	10	5
D. It takes too much time					
General public	28	22	24	14	12
Business owners	28	26	26	11	9
E. It requires lots of education					
General public	11	13	37	22	16
Business owners	6	14	38	26	17

Note: [a]"Using a five-point scale, where '5' means you strongly agree (SA), and '1' means that you strongly disagree (SD), do you think people do not go into business because:" [2]

Most of the responses given by the general public in Nebraska to the major reasons why other people do not start a business are roughly consistent with those of small business owners in Nebraska. The general public gives less weight to risk-taking propensity (74% agreement) than do small business owners (82% agreement). The general public attached equal importance as business owners in terms of agreement to the monetary requirement (75% agreement) and the time demand (50% agreement) factor as major reasons people do not start a business. The general public is less likely (41% agreement) than business owners to think that management concerns are a major reason for not starting a business. They also give more weight to education (24%) as a barrier to entrepreneurship than do business owners, although most of the respondents in both groups recognize that a lack of education is not necessarily a major hindrance to starting a business.

The other item was open ended and let the general public supply reasons for why they did not want to start a business (Table 4.13). In this case, the question sought a more personal answer and took into account individual circumstances or experiences that affected the entrepreneurial decision rather than asking why other people did not start a business. The answers to the questions came from the half (51%) of the 2,460 members of the general public in Nebraska who stated they were not interested in starting a business in the 2005 survey (see Table 4.1 for the question). The question was not asked of the general public in the 2006 survey.

Table 4.13: Major Reason Not to Start Own Business[a]

Response	General Public (n=1,430)[b]
Age (too young or too old)	39%
Lack of energy/time/skills/ideas	19
Like current situation (education/job)	12
Problems with managing the business	9
Not enough money/financial capital	8
It is too risky	7
Other	5
None	1
Don't know/Refused	1

Notes:
[a]"What is the major reason you might NOT want to start a business of your own?" [1]
[b]Those responding "no" to wanting to start own business (see Table 4.1).

The major reason for not wanting to be an entrepreneur according to this group was the age factor. This predominant response was that individuals thought they were either too young or too old for entrepreneurship (39%). Given the demographics in Nebraska, it was probably because they thought they were too old to start a business.[6] Entrepreneurship is generally considered an undertaking of younger rather than older adults.

The next general factor for not wanting to start a business cited by almost two in ten (19%) of Nebraskans was the lack of energy, time, skills, or ideas. Other problems that concerned the general public were the problems of managing the business (9%), not having sufficient financial capital (8%), or worries about the business risk (7%). What is instructive about many of these concerns is that they can be addressed through educational programs that prepare people for entrepreneurship. It may be the lack of exposure to such an education in entrepreneurship that is contributing to the deficiencies that people express in areas such as ideas, skills, energy, or time. There may not be anything that can be done about the age factor or even satisfaction with a current situation (cited by 12%), but the other reasons given for not starting a business could be addressed through more education and mentoring, and thus increase the pool of potential entrepreneurs in Nebraska.

COMPARISONS: COMMUNITY COLLEGE REGIONS, BUSINESS SIZES, AND NATIONAL

The procedures for the collection of the survey data permit the data to be analyzed by the six community college districts or regions in Nebraska: Metropolitan, Southeast, Central, Northeast, Mid-Plains, and Western (see Figure 2.4 for the district map).[7] A question to be answered is whether there is substantial variation in the survey responses among the six regions for the general public survey items that were discussed in this chapter. To address this question, the detailed responses to each survey item are provided at the end of this chapter in Appendix 4A.

The general conclusion is that there are only limited differences in the responses for the general public based on community college district. This conclusion applies to those items related to interest in entrepreneurship and reasons and challenges to starting a business that were included in this chapter. The differences by region are minor and within the margin of sampling error. For example, more than four in ten (43%) of the general public in Nebraska said they were interested in entrepreneurship (see Table 4.1). The interest in entrepreneurship within each district was similar because it ranged from 40 percent in the southeast and northeast districts to 46 percent in the metropolitan and western districts (Table 4.1a).

Another question to be asked is whether there are important differences in responses among business owners based on the size of the firm they own. Firm size in this case is measured by the number of employees. Four sizes of firms by number of employees were considered: 1–10, 11–20, 21–49, and 50 or more).[8] The tables showing the breakdown by firm size for all business owner items in the chapter are reported in Appendix 4B.

The tabular data show that most of the response differences by firm size are minor for each of the questions. For example, when asked for the major reason for wanting to start a business about six in ten (from 60% to 63%) in each group stated that it was to "be my own boss" (Table 4.8b). For a few items, the views of the smallest firms (1 to 10 employees) differ from those of the largest firms (20 or more employees) such as with satisfaction with entrepreneurship (Tables 4.4b and 4.5b) or reasons that other people want to become entrepreneurs (Table 4.7b). These differences, however, are only suggestive, and the small sample size makes it difficult to assess their importance.

A third question to be answered is whether the views of the general public in Nebraska or its business owners are substantially different than the views of the general public or business owners based on national samples. In 2002, a survey was conducted by Gallup of 607 members of the general public and 403 owners of business firms that employed fewer than 50 workers. Many of the questions that were asked on this national survey were also asked in the Nebraska surveys, making it possible to conduct a comparison of the national and state results on selected survey items as shown in the tables in Appendix 4C.[9]

As for interest in entrepreneurship, it may be somewhat less in Nebraska (43%) than nationwide (55%) (Table 4.1c), but the conclusion is a mixed one. General interest in entrepreneurship is composed of two types: individuals who said they were interested in starting their own business, but had not yet started one, and individuals who said they had already started a business. When the percentages are divided into these categories, fewer Nebraskans than the national sample (32% versus 48%) say yes to entrepreneurship among those who have not yet started a business, probably because the average age of the general public in Nebraska is slightly older than the nationwide sample (46 versus 44 years old). A larger proportion of Nebraskans (11%) also say they have already started a business compared with national sample (7%), suggesting that more Nebraskans than adults nationwide may be more willing to act on their entrepreneurial interest.

In most other respects, the responses of the general public in Nebraska are quite similar to those from the general public nationwide. Many Nebraskans, as do adults nationwide, think that the major reason people start a business is to be their own boss, build something for the family, or to use their skills and abilities, and few think that it is to overcome a challenge (Table 4.8c). In fact, when the sample of those interested in starting a business from each survey group is asked the reason why, about equivalent percentages from (51% in Nebraska and 48% nationwide) gave the same response, which was to "be my own boss." The responses from the two groups also were similar in their opinions about the various challenges to starting a business (Table 4.10c) on such matters as costs, sales, financing, competition, business ideas, and government regulation.

The responses of business owners in Nebraska and nationwide are about the same to questions asked of each group. Over half of each group said they first thought about starting a business when they were 29 years old or younger (Table 4.3c). Over three-fourths from each group also expressed a high degree of satisfaction with entrepreneurship and prefer it over working for someone else (Table 4.5c). Serial entrepreneurs, those who start more than one business, are found in Nebraska in about the same proportion as in the nation (Table 4.6c). Business owners in Nebraska and nationally hold about the same opinions about the reasons for entrepreneurship (Table 4.7c) and challenges to entrepreneurship (Table 4.10c).

CONCLUSIONS

The results to this portion of the survey questions provide extensive insights about the entrepreneurial thinking of the general public and small business owners in Nebraska. Some of the key points from the survey data can be summarized in the following statements.

- There is substantial interest in starting a business among the general public in Nebraska. This interest is greatest among the younger adults in the state, many of whom say they are likely to act on this idea to start a business.
- Entrepreneurship in Nebraska is often a multiple event because once a small business owner has started a business, he or she is very likely to start another one.
- Entrepreneurship is viewed as a good career as indicated by the fact that the great majority of both the general public and small business owners in Nebraska say they would want their child to become an entrepreneur.
- A primary reason that people become entrepreneurs is to be their own boss and not just to make money. This need for freedom and control was a dominant factor driving people to become entrepreneurs.
- There are many challenges and obstacles to entrepreneurship, some of which involve management, education, risk, or economic factors. An unexpected and major challenge for business owners in Nebraska was learning how to handle government regulation and red tape.
- The differences in the item responses are relatively minor across the six community college districts in Nebraska, by size of firm, and for state and national comparisons.

The general conclusion to be drawn is that there is great potential for expansion of entrepreneurship in Nebraska because the climate for it is positive. Young adults in Nebraska are interested in starting a business and they are likely to act on this idea if they have the necessary education and community support to achieve their goals. The general public is supportive of entrepreneurship despite its many challenges. Business owners are most appreciative of the economic opportunity and freedom entrepreneurship offers, and see those factors as prime motivators. Nebraska can benefit from this positive climate if ways can be found to capitalize on it because it may lead to more entrepreneurial activity in the state.

NOTES

1. Most of the survey questions were based on ones developed by Walstad and another colleague for other national studies (Walstad and Kourilsky, 1996; Walstad and Kourilsky, 1998a; Kourilsky and Walstad, 1998a; Walstad and Kourilsky, 1999; Kourilsky and Walstad, 2000; Kourilsky and Walstad, 2002; Kourilsky and Walstad, 2005; and Kourilsky and Walstad, 2007). A few questions also were prepared by Eric Thompson and Amy Thomas. Glenn Phelps of Gallup supervised preparation of the survey and oversaw work on data collection.

2. In 2005 and again in 2006, the sample plan for the Nebraska general public was designed to achieve 400 completes from each of the six Nebraska community college regions: Western; Mid-Plains; Northeastern; Central; Southeast; and Metropolitan. A random digit dial procedure was employed that divided telephone number prefixes into the appropriate regions. In some cases telephone prefix numbers occurred in more than one community college region. In those cases the respondent was asked to identify the closest community college and their response determined the region. Potential numbers for each region were generated, randomized, and divided into replicates of 25. Each number in the replicate was worked until resolution under a three-call design. Calls were made during weekday evenings and weekend days and evenings. In 2005, calling was conducted between October 6 and November 1, 2005. A total of 2,460 completes were achieved with a gross completion rate of 19.1 percent and a cooperation rate of 90.6 percent. In 2006, calling was conducted between December 6 and December 12, 2006. A total of 2,475 completes were achieved with a cooperation rate of 92.6 percent. For both years, the data were weighted to reflect population statistics at state level and at the regional level. Margin of sampling error at a 95 percent confidence level for the entire sample each year is approximately plus or minus (+/–) 2.0 and (+/–) 4.91

for each of the groups. The results from the entire sample are reported in the chapter text. The results by community college district are found in Appendix 4A.

3. In 2005 and again in 2006, the sample plan for Nebraska business owners was designed to provide 600 total completes, 150 each from four strata based on employee size: 1 to 10, 11–19, 20–49, and 50–100. A list of Nebraska businesses with fewer than 100 employees was obtained from a national supplier. Some SIC codes were excluded from the sample, including 86 nonprofits, 91–97 government, and 82 education. The list was randomized and divided into replicates of 25. Each piece of sample in a replicate was worked until resolution in a five-call design. In 2005, calling was conducted between October 6 and November 1, 2005. The quota of 150 completes was met in the three business groups with less than 50 employees. Only 103 completes, however, were obtained from businesses of 50 to 100 employees due to insufficient sample size. The total completes were 555. In 2006, calling was conducted between November 22 and December 4, 2006. The quota of 150 completes was met in the three business groups with less than 50 employees. Only 126 completes were obtained from businesses of 50 to 100 employees due to insufficient sample size. The total completes were 578, but 11 cases were eliminated because the business had no employees. For each year, the results were weighted so statewide statistics reflected the correct percentage of business from each of the sample groups. Margin of sampling error is approximately plus or minus (+/–) 4.16 at 95 percent level of confidence for the total and ranges from approximately plus or minus (+/–) 8.03 to 9.85 for each of the groups. The results from the total sample of business owners are found in the chapter text. The results by number of employees per firm are found in Appendix 4B.

4. Given the similarity in the sample sizes for the two years, the maximum margin of sampling error was essentially the same for those survey items that were asked in only one of the two years. In those cases the sampling error was plus or minus (+/-) 2.0 percentage points for the general public and plus or minus (+/-) 4.16 percentage points for small business owners. For those items that were asked both years, the sample size used to calculate the sampling error essentially doubled, so the sampling error was smaller. In those cases, the maximum margin of sampling error was approximately plus or minus (+/-) 1.4 percentage points for the general public and approximately plus or minus (+/-) 2.9 percentage points for small business owners.

5. At the end of each question for each table is a code in square brackets: The [1] refers to items given only in the 2005 survey. The code [2] refers to items given only in the 2006 survey. The code [3] refers to a survey given both years. If a survey was given to one group but not another in a particular year, the code includes a symbol for either the

general public (P) or small business owners (B) to indicate that group distinction for a survey item.

6. Based on U.S. Census data for Nebraska in 2006, there were 1.27 million people in the state who were 20 years of age or older. Of this population, 33 percent were 55 years of age or older, which is an age range at which most people are either considering retirement or are retired.

7. See note 2 for a description of the procedures used for data collection and estimates of the margins for sampling error by community college district.

8. See note 3 for a description of procedures used for data collection and estimates for the margins for sampling error with the business owner sample.

9. A description of the national samples and the survey procedures used by Gallup to collect the data is found in Kourilsky and Walstad (2007, pp. 11–15). Two basic differences between the national and Nebraska surveys should be noted. First, the Nebraska surveys were conducted in 2005 and 2006 and the national surveys were conducted in 2002. Although the time frames for the surveys differ, there has not been a significant change in the conditions for entrepreneurship from 2002 to 2005 or 2006 (Fairlie, 2007), and the views and opinions of the general public and business owners about entrepreneurship appear to be stable over time (Kourilsky and Walstad, 2007, pp. 112–129). Second, the size of firms by the number of employees is smaller in the national sample (fewer than 50) than in the Nebraska sample (100 or less). This difference, however, is minimal because 98.8 percent of the weighted responses for Nebraska came from small business owners with 49 or fewer employees compared with 100 percent for the national sample.

APPENDIX 4A: General Public by Community College

Table 4.1a: Want to Start Own Business[a] (n=4,935)

	Community College District					
	Metro-politan	South-East	Central	North-east	Mid-Plains	Western
Response	(n=819)	(801)	(807)	(827)	(858)	(823)
	%	%	%	%	%	%
Yes	37	30	31	28	26	30
Already have own business	9	10	11	12	15	16
Total for entrepreneurship	**46**	**40**	**42**	**40**	**41**	**46**
No	53	58	58	59	58	53
Don't know/Refused	1	2	1	1	1	1

Note: [a]"Do you think you would want to start a business of your own?" [3]

Table 4.2a: Likely to Act on Idea to Start Own Business[a] (n=1,502)[b]

	Community College District					
	Metro-politan	South-east	Central	North-East	Mid-Plains	Western
Response	(n=303)	(243)	(249)	(235)	(225)	(247)
	%	%	%	%	%	%
5 Very likely	27	22	24	24	27	25
4	17	25	15	23	17	19
3	31	24	32	26	35	33
2	14	16	17	18	12	12
1 Not at all likely	11	13	11	9	9	11
Don't know/Refused	0	0	1	0	0	0

Notes:
[a]"Using a five-point scale, where 5 is very likely, and 1 is not at all likely, how likely are you to act on this idea to start your own business?" [3]
[b]For YES respondents on whether you'd want to start a business of your own (see Table 4.1a).

Table 4.4a: Child Become an Entrepreneur[a] (n=1,018)

	Community College District					
	Metro-politan	South-east	Central	North-East	Mid-Plains	Western
Response	(n=186)	(153)	(165)	(163)	(165)	(186)
	%	%	%	%	%	%
Yes	91	92	92	94	90	90
No	7	4	5	3	7	8
Don't know/Refused	2	5	3	3	3	2

Note: [a]"Would you want your child to become an entrepreneur?" [1]

Table 4.7a: Reasons People Go into Business[a] (n=4,935)

Reasons	SA	A	U	D	SD
	%	%	%	%	%
A. To be their own boss					
Metropolitan CC (n=819)	74	18	4	2	1
Southeast CC (n=801)	68	22	7	1	2
Central CC (n=807)	66	23	7	2	3
Northeast CC (n=827)	66	22	7	1	3
Mid-Plains CC (n=858)	72	20	6	1	1
Western CC (n=823)	67	22	8	2	2
B. To build something for their family					
Metropolitan CC	58	27	12	2	1
Southeast CC	52	33	11	2	2
Central CC	57	28	12	2	2
Northeast CC	59	27	10	3	2
Mid-Plains CC	58	28	11	1	2
Western CC	58	28	11	2	1
C. To use their skills and abilities					
Metropolitan CC	55	29	13	1	1
Southeast CC	49	34	11	4	2
Central CC	48	37	12	2	2
Northeast CC	50	31	13	2	2
Mid-Plains CC	49	33	13	3	1
Western CC	51	33	13	2	2
D. To earn lots of money					
Metropolitan CC	36	26	29	6	4
Southeast CC	32	28	28	7	5
Central CC	34	25	31	7	3
Northeast CC	35	24	28	8	5
Mid-Plains CC	31	24	33	7	5
Western CC	30	25	33	8	4
E. To overcome a challenge					
Metropolitan CC	21	24	33	15	6
Southeast CC	19	25	35	12	6
Central CC	19	24	38	12	6
Northeast CC	21	24	35	12	7
Mid-Plains CC	19	24	34	14	8
Western CC	22	22	34	13	8

Note: [a]"Using a five-point scale, where "5" means you strongly agree (SA), and "1" means that you strongly disagree (SD), do you think people go into business:" [3]

Table 4.8a: Major Reason for Wanting to Start Business[a] (n=1,021)[b]

	Community College District					
Response	Metro-politan (n=188)	South-east (154)	Central (165)	North-East (163)	Mid-Plains (163)	Western (186)
	%	%	%	%	%	%
To be my own boss	46	42	49	46	48	43
To build something for their family	7	9	3	6	6	8
To help the community/ Provide jobs	3	7	10	8	7	5
To use my skills and abilities	11	12	15	12	13	18
To earn lots of money	22	14	15	20	15	17
To overcome a challenge	5	4	4	1	5	7
Other	1	1	1	4	2	0
Don't know/Refused	0	0	0	1	1	0

Notes:
[a]"What is the major reason you might want to start a business of your own?" [1]
[b]Those responding "Yes" to wanting to start own business plus those already owning a business (see Table 4.1a).

Table 4.10a: More Difficult Challenges in Starting a Business[a] (n=2,460)

	Community College District					
Response	Metro-politan (n=419)	South-east (399)	Central (408)	North-east (412)	Mid-Plains (404)	Western (419)
	%	%	%	%	%	%
Handling government regulation and red tape	75	81	77	74	74	74
Controlling costs	84	83	85	82	83	87
Developing sales	81	80	81	84	82	81
Obtaining loans and financing	76	73	75	76	74	75
Competing with other businesses	84	80	83	76	75	80
Coming up with good ideas	61	64	67	72	61	61

Note: [a]"Which of the following challenges do you think prove to be more difficult than initially anticipated by people who start a new business?" [1]

Table 4.12a: Reasons People Do Not Start a Business[a] *(n=2,475)*

Reasons	SA	A	U	D	SD
	%	%	%	%	%
A. It is too risky					
Metropolitan CC (n=400)	50	25	17	4	4
Southeast CC (n=402)	47	32	12	5	4
Central CC (n=400)	46	27	18	5	5
Northeast CC (n=415)	43	25	20	8	4
Mid-Plains CC (n=454)	38	32	20	6	4
Western CC (n=404)	39	32	19	6	3
B. It requires too much money					
Metropolitan CC	49	24	17	5	4
Southeast CC	48	26	16	4	4
Central CC	49	28	16	4	2
Northeast CC	51	26	15	3	4
Mid-Plains CC	50	26	16	5	3
Western CC	53	23	15	5	4
C. It is difficult to manage people					
Metropolitan CC	17	23	34	14	11
Southeast CC	21	20	34	16	7
Central CC	19	25	33	14	10
Northeast CC	19	19	37	14	8
Mid-Plains CC	17	25	35	12	10
Western CC	22	20	34	16	8
D. It takes too much time					
Metropolitan CC	32	22	21	14	12
Southeast CC	30	21	25	14	10
Central CC	21	21	25	16	17
Northeast CC	25	25	26	13	11
Mid-Plains CC	26	21	26	13	13
Western CC	23	21	28	12	15
E. It requires lots of education					
Metropolitan CC	12	12	34	24	18
Southeast CC	10	12	37	23	16
Central CC	9	16	39	20	16
Northeast CC	13	17	41	14	15
Mid-Plains CC	12	15	35	24	13
Western CC	10	12	37	27	13

Note: [a]"Using a five-point scale, where '5' means you strongly agree (SA), and '1' means that you strongly disagree (SD), do you think people do not go into business because:" [2]

Table 4.13a: Major Reason Not to Start Own Business[a] (n=1,430)[b]

Response	Community College District					
	Metro-politan (n=230)	South-east (243)	Central (242)	North-East (248)	Mid-Plains (237)	Western (230)
	%	%	%	%	%	%
Age (too old or too young)	35	35	42	48	47	48
Lack of energy/time/skills/ ideas	18	19	20	19	16	14
Like current situation (education/job)	11	16	12	8	15	12
Problems with managing the business	10	8	9	8	7	5
Not enough money/financial capital	8	8	9	7	6	10
It is too risky	7	8	4	5	3	7
Other	7	3	4	5	5	3
None	2	2	0	0	0	1
Don't know/Refused	2	1	0	0	1	0

Notes:
[a]"What is the major reason you might NOT want to start a business of your own?" [1]
[b]Those responding "no" to wanting to start own business (see Table 4.1a).

APPENDIX 4B: Business Owners by Number of Employees

Table 4.3b: Age When Thought of Starting Own Business[a] (n=1,122)

	Number of Employees			
	1–10	**11–19**	**20–49**	**50–100**
Response	(n=322)	(314)	(296)	(190)
	%	%	%	%
Younger than 18 years old	15	12	14	13
18–29	50	45	46	52
30–39	19	26	25	19
40–49	9	12	9	9
50+	8	5	6	7

Note: [a]"How old were you when you first thought about starting or owning your own business?" [3]

Table 4.4b: Child Become an Entrepreneur[a] (n=555)

	Number of Employees			
	1–10	**11–19**	**20–49**	**50–100**
Response	(n=150)	(152)	(179)	(74)
	%	%	%	%
Yes	80	84	90	84
No	13	12	8	11
Don't know/Refused	6	5	2	5

Note: [a]"Would you want your child to become an entrepreneur?" [1]

Table 4.5b: Start Own Business or Work for Someone Else[a] (n=567)

	Number of Employees			
	1–10	**11–19**	**20–49**	**50–100**
Response	(n=172)	(162)	(146)	(87)
	%	%	%	%
Starting own business	78	81	86	84
Working for someone else	18	17	10	14
Don't know/Refused/Other	5	2	4	2

Note: [a]"If you had a choice between: (1) starting your own business, or (2) working for someone else who owns a business, which would you rather do?" [2]

Table 4.6b: Number of Other Businesses Started[a] *(n=555)*

	Number of Employees			
	1–10	**11–19**	**20–49**	**50–100**
Response	(n=150)	(152)	(179)	(74)
	%	**%**	**%**	**%**
None other than this one	33	28	24	25
1	29	30	30	29
2	22	21	19	23
3 or more	16	21	37	24

Note: [a]"In addition to this business, how many businesses have you ever started or owned?" [1]

Table 4.7b: Reasons People Go into Business[a] *(n=567)*

Reasons	SA	A	U	D	SD
	%	**%**	**%**	**%**	**%**
A. To be their own boss					
1–10 employees (n=172)	74	15	10	1	1
11–19 employees (n=162)	67	22	7	3	1
20–49 employees (n=146)	71	21	4	3	1
50–100 employees (n=87)	71	23	5	1	0
B. To build something for their family					
1–10 employees	62	26	10	1	1
11–19 employees	48	31	17	4	1
20–49 employees	56	30	11	2	1
50–100 employees	51	38	10	1	0
C. To use their skills and abilities					
1–10 employees	58	28	13	1	0
11–19 employees	52	33	12	1	3
20–49 employees	49	37	10	3	1
50–100 employees	48	37	10	5	0
D. To earn lots of money					
1–10 employees	30	22	37	5	6
11–19 employees	29	29	28	9	6
20–49 employees	36	30	23	7	5
50–100 employees	25	38	30	7	0
E. To overcome a challenge					
1–10 employees	20	29	30	14	7
11–19 employees	19	29	32	17	4
20–49 employees	18	30	32	14	6
50–100 employees	17	30	35	8	10

Note: [a]"Using a five-point scale, where '5' means you strongly agree (SA), and '1' means that you strongly disagree (SD), do you think people go into business:" [2]

Table 4.8b: Major Reason for Wanting to Start Business[a] *(n=555)*

	Number of Employees			
	1–10	**11–19**	**20–49**	**50–100**
Response	(n=150)	(152)	(179)	(74)
	%	**%**	**%**	**%**
To be my own boss	63	63	60	62
To build something for their family	13	9	11	11
To help the community/Provide jobs	7	9	9	7
To use my skills and abilities	9	7	5	0
To earn lots of money	5	9	7	10
To overcome a challenge	3	3	5	7
Other	0	1	0	0
Don't know/Refused	1	1	3	4

Note: [a]"What is the major reason why you wanted to start and/or own a business?" [1]

Table 4.9b: Event or Experience Prompting Business Start[a] *(n=555)*

	Number of Employees			
	1–10	**11–19**	**20–49**	**50–100**
Response	(n=150)	(152)	(179)	(74)
	%	**%**	**%**	**%**
Economic Freedom/Job Related Issues	**35**	**39**	**39**	**38**
1. Need for independence/Be own boss	14	13	17	19
2. Past job or job experience	6	11	10	11
3. Dissatisfaction with job/job burnout	7	10	8	3
4. Losing a job or becoming unemployed	5	4	3	5
5. Needed money	3	1	1	0
Economic Opportunity/Conditions	**31**	**33**	**33**	**30**
1. Spotted a viable idea or opportunity	22	27	30	29
2. Market/Demand conditions were right	9	6	3	1
Other Experiences	**27**	**27**	**22**	**21**
1. Events or experience in family	22	23	17	18
2. Courses or educational experiences	2	4	4	3
3. Hobbies	3	0	1	0
Other	**1**	**0**	**1**	**1**
Don't know/Refused	**5**	**2**	**6**	**10**

Note: [a]"In retrospect, what was the first significant event or experience that prompted you to start or own this business?" [1]

Table 4.10b: More Difficult Challenges in Starting a Business[a] (n=555)

Challenges	Number of Employees			
	1–10 (n=150)	11–19 (152)	20–49 (179)	50–100 (74)
	%	%	%	%
Handling gov. regulation and red tape	79	76	78	84
Controlling costs	77	84	78	76
Developing sales	69	66	67	64
Obtaining loans and financing	63	54	57	55
Competing with other businesses	61	63	58	55
Coming up with good ideas	46	46	44	32

Note: [a]"Which of the following challenges do you think prove to be more difficult than initially anticipated by people who start a new business?" [1]

Table 4.11b: Greatest Non-Financial Obstacle[a] (n=555)

Response	Number of Employees			
	1–10 (n=150)	11–19 (152)	20–49 (179)	50–100 (74)
	%	%	%	%
A. Management Factors	**45**	**37**	**55**	**56**
Developing clientele	17	5	10	15
Handling government regulations	13	9	13	11
Concerns about managing and motivating people	9	16	25	27
Coming up with a good idea or opportunity	6	7	7	3
B. Risk—Being able to handle it	**16**	**15**	**8**	**10**
C. Economic Conditions	**14**	**18**	**9**	**11**
Poor economic conditions	6	11	5	7
Location	5	3	3	3
Competition	3	4	1	1
D. Education Factors	**13**	**16**	**13**	**8**
Young age or lack of experience	5	6	6	3
Lack of education and skills	5	8	5	4
Lack of personal knowledge about technology	3	2	2	1
Other	**3**	**7**	**3**	**4**
None	**1**	**3**	**1**	**3**
Don't know/Refused	**7**	**5**	**10**	**10**

Note: [a]"Other than financing, what do you think was your greatest obstacle to starting your current business?" [1]

Table 4.12b: Reasons People Do Not Start a Business[a] *(n=567)*

Reasons	SA	A	U	D	SD
	%	%	%	%	%
A. It is too risky					
1–10 employees (n=172)	52	30	10	5	4
11–19 employees (n=162)	53	22	17	4	4
20–49 employees (n=146)	51	23	16	5	5
50–100 employees (n=87)	47	32	16	2	2
B. It requires too much money					
1–10 employees	48	29	16	5	2
11–19 employees	49	28	17	5	1
20–49 employees	41	30	21	2	6
50–100 employees	44	30	20	6	1
C. It is difficult to manage people					
1–10 employees	31	28	27	9	4
11–19 employees	37	27	22	9	5
20–49 employees	33	30	24	8	6
50–100 employees	23	35	25	13	5
D. It takes too much time					
1–10 employees	29	27	24	12	9
11–19 employees	30	25	23	14	8
20–49 employees	30	22	26	12	10
50–100 employees	20	25	31	14	10
E. It requires lots of education					
1–10 employees	7	15	37	25	16
11–19 employees	6	7	41	28	19
20–49 employees	8	10	37	28	16
50–100 employees	2	10	51	21	16

Note: [a]"Using a five-point scale, where '5' means you strongly agree (SA), and '1' means that you strongly disagree (SD), do you think people do not go into business because:" [2]

APPENDIX 4C: Nebraska vs. United States Data

Table 4.1c: Want to Start Own Business[a]

Response	Nebraska (n=4,935)	U.S. (n=607)
	%	%
Yes	32	48
Already have own business	11	7
Total of those interested in entrepreneurship	**43**	**55**
No	3	5

Note: [a]"Do you think you would want to start a business of your own?" [3]

Table 4.2c: Likely to Act on Idea to Start Own Business[a, b]

Response	Nebraska (n=1,225)	U.S. (n=281)
	%	%
5 Very likely	25	37
4	19	16
3	29	25
2	15	10
1 Not at all likely	11	13

Notes:
[a]"Using a five-point scale, where 5 is very likely, and 1 is not at all likely, how likely are you to act on this idea to start your own business?" [3]
[b]For YES respondents on whether you'd want to start a business of your own (see Table 4.1c).

Table 4.3c: Age When Thought of Starting Own Business[a]

Response	Nebraska (n=1,122)	U.S. (n=403)
	%	%
Younger than 18 years old	14	10
18–29	50	44
30–39	20	28
40–49	9	13
50+	5	6

Note: [a]"How old were you when you first thought about starting or owning your own business?" [3]

Table 4.5c: Start Own Business or Work for Someone Else[a]

Response	Nebraska (n=567)	U.S. (n=403)
	%	%
Starting own business	77	85
Working for someone else	29	10
Don't know/Refused	5	5

Note: [a]"If you had a choice between: (1) starting your own business, or (2) working for someone else who owns a business, which would you rather do?" [2]

Table 4.6c: Number of Other Businesses Started[a]

Response	Nebraska (n=555)	U.S. (n=403)
	%	%
None other than this one	33	33
1	29	24
2	22	17
3 or more	16	26

Note: [a]"In addition to this business, how many businesses have you ever started or owned?" [1]

Table 4.7c: Reasons People Go into Business[a]

Reasons	SA	A	U	D	SD
	%	%	%	%	%
A. To be their own boss					
Nebraska General Public (n=4,935)	70	21	6	2	2
U.S. General Public (n=607)	75	14	7	3	2
Nebraska Business Owners (n=567)	72	16	10	1	1
U.S. Business Owners (n=403)	70	19	9	1	1
B. To build something for their family					
Nebraska General Public	57	29	12	2	2
U.S. General Public	59	21	15	3	2
Nebraska Business Owners	62	25	10	2	1
U.S. Business Owners	51	22	21	6	2
C. To use their skills and abilities					
Nebraska General Public	51	33	13	2	2
U.S. General Public	53	25	15	5	2
Nebraska Business Owners	58	28	13	1	0
U.S. Business Owners	56	22	16	3	2
D. To earn lots of money					
Nebraska General Public	34	26	30	7	4
U.S. General Public	49	20	22	5	4
Nebraska Business Owners	30	22	35	6	7
U.S. Business Owners	38	19	29	11	3
E. To overcome a challenge					
Nebraska General Public	20	24	35	13	7
U.S. General Public	26	23	29	13	7
Nebraska Business Owners	21	29	30	13	8
U.S. Business Owners	27	18	35	12	6

Note: [a]"Using a five-point scale, where '5' means you strongly agree (SA), and '1' means that you strongly disagree (SD), do you think people go into business:" [3P, 2B]

Table 4.8c: Major Reason for Wanting to Start Business[a, b]

	General Public		Business Owners	
	Nebr.	**U.S.**	**Nebr.**	**U.S.**
Response	(n=1,021)	(281)	(555)	(403)
	%	**%**	**%**	**%**
To be my own boss	51	48	63	56
To build something for their family	7	6	13	8
To help the community/Provide jobs	6	4	7	–
To use my skills and abilities	13	9	8	15
To earn lots of money	18	18	6	9
To overcome a challenge	5	5	3	4
Other	1	8	–	8
Don't know/Refused	0	1	1	0

Notes:
[a]For the General Public, the question was: "What is the major reason you might want to start a business of your own?" For Business Owners, the question was: "What is the major reason why you wanted to start and/or own a business?" [1]
[b]Those responding "Yes" to wanting to start own business plus those already owning a business (see Table 4.1c).

Table 4.10c: More Difficult Challenges in Starting a Business[a]

	General Public		Business Owners	
	Nebr.	**U.S.**	**Nebr.**	**U.S.**
Response	(n=1,208)	(281)	(555)	(403)
	%	**%**	**%**	**%**
Handling gov. regulation and red tape	77	71	79	71
Controlling costs	84	81	78	77
Developing sales	81	78	69	72
Obtaining loans and financing	75	75	62	60
Competing with other businesses	81	79	61	58
Coming up with good ideas	64	61	46	54

Note: [a]"Which of the following challenges do you think prove to be more difficult than initially anticipated by people who start a new business?" [1]

Table 4.13c: Major Reason Not to Start Own Business[a, b]

Response	Nebraska (n=1,430)	U.S. (n=283)
	%	%
Age (too young or too old)	39	24
Lack of energy/time/skills/ideas	19	24
Like current situation (education/job)	12	11
Problems with managing the business	9	9
Not enough money/financial capital	8	8
It is too risky	7	9
Other	5	14
None	1	–
Don't know/Refused	1	2

Notes:
[a]"What is the major reason you might NOT want to start a business of your own?" [1]
[b]Those responding "no" to wanting to start own business (see Table 4.1c).

CHAPTER 5

Perspectives on Knowledge and Education

What people know about entrepreneurship and their education for entrepreneurship can have a strong influence on their attitudes toward starting a business or the overall climate of support for entrepreneurship. For these reasons, the knowledge and education dimensions for entrepreneurship are important topics for study with the general public and business owners in Nebraska. This chapter, therefore, continues the survey analysis started in the previous chapter, but offers a general assessment of the entrepreneurial understanding based on responses to test questions and self-ratings of knowledge. The chapter also provides a detailed reporting on the role of education in preparing people for launching new businesses and what people consider to be the value of entrepreneurship education at different levels.

ENTREPRENEURIAL KNOWLEDGE

The survey included five questions for assessing basic knowledge about small business and entrepreneurship. The multiple-choice questions were a small sample of many possible ones that could have been asked of the general public in Nebraska. Each question was analyzed for insights into each group's knowledge, and not just their opinions, about small business and entrepreneurship.

The first question was easy and asked the general public in Nebraska to select a correct description of an entrepreneur – a person who starts a business (Table 5.1). Nine in ten (91%) Nebraskans selected the correct answer. Less than one in ten thought it was the manager of a large corporation (5%) or something else. This question was asked to check if most people had a solid understanding of what an entrepreneur was, given that the term is not commonly used.

Table 5.1: Description of Entrepreneur[a]

Response	General Public (n=2,460)
A person who starts a business[b]	91%
A manager of a large corporation	5
A government official running a regulatory agency	1
Some/combination/all	1
Don't know/Refused	2

Notes:
[a]"Which of the following best describes an entrepreneur?" [1][1]
[b]Correct response

Small business has been responsible for creating the most new jobs in the economy over the past ten years (Table 5.2). People often are not aware of the major contribution that small business makes to communities by creating jobs because most of the focus of business news tends to be on larger corporations with brand names. As expected, Nebraskans found this question about entrepreneurship to be even more challenging. Just half (50%) of Nebraskans were aware of the contribution small business makes to jobs creation. Over a third (37%) attributed most jobs creation to large businesses and one in ten (10%) thought it was the Federal government.

Table 5.2: Who Created Most New Jobs in Past Ten Years[a]

Response	General Public (n=2,460)
Small businesses[b]	50%
Large businesses	37
The Federal government	10
Don't know/Refused	3

Notes:
[a]"Over the last ten years, which of the following groups has created the most new jobs in the economy?" [1]
[b]Correct response

A third question asked which factor was most important for business survival (Table 5.3). The list of incorrect answers included having a board of directors, the value of the company's common stock, and having a low rate of depreciation. The correct answer, the company's cash flow, was selected by almost seven in ten (68%). Cash flow is most critical for the survival of a business because if a company does not generate sufficient revenue to pay its bills, then it faces the prospect of bankruptcy. Most Nebraskans recognized the essential contribution of cash flow to the continuation of a business.

Table 5.3: Most Important Factor for Business Survival[a]

Response	General Public (n=4,935)
The company's cash flow[b]	68%
The value of the company's common stock	11
Having a board of directors	6
Having a low depreciation rate	8
Some/combination/all	3
Don't know/Refused	5

Notes:
[a]"Which factor is most important for business survival?" [3]
[b]Correct response

Economic knowledge serves as a foundation for entrepreneurial understanding. To assess this dimension, the survey included a fourth question asking how the prices of most products are determined in a market economy (Table 5.4). In competitive markets, the prices of products are established by the supply of and demand for products. In such cases, it is the

Table 5.4: Determination of Prices[a]

Response	General Public (n=2,475)
Supply and demand for products[b]	67%
Local, state, or Federal government	9
The Consumer Price Index	9
Monetary policy of the Federal Reserve	4
Some/combination/all	5
Don't know/Refused	6

Notes:
[a]"To the best of your knowledge, the prices of most products in a competitive market, like the United States, are determined by?" [2]
[b]Correct response

competition among buyers and sellers of a product and not some government or institution that allocates resources and determines the prices for products. The results show that two-thirds (67%) of the general public in Nebraska knew the prices of most products in a market economy like the United States were determined by the forces of supply and demand. The other third had serious misperceptions about how a market economy works. Almost one in ten (9%) responded that the prices were determined by the local, state, or Federal government. A same proportion (9%) stated the prices of most products were determined by a measure of inflation – the consumer price index. A few respondents (4%) thought that prices in competitive markets were set by the monetary policy of the Federal Reserve.

A question on profit was included as the fifth knowledge item on the survey to investigate if the general public in Nebraska understood its role in a market economy (Table 5.5). The basic purpose of profit is to serve as a reward to entrepreneurs for discovering market opportunities that will benefit consumers and for taking the risk to produce those products for consumers. On this question, the general public in Nebraska showed the lowest level of understanding. A third (34%) thought it was to pay for the wages and salaries of workers. Sixteen percent (16%) stated that the purpose of profit was to transfer income to the wealthy. Less than one in ten either gave some other response (5%) or did not know (4%). Thus, about six in ten (59%) of the general public in Nebraska view profit as some mechanism for redistribution to serve either workers or the wealthy, or simply had no clear idea. Only about four in ten (41%) recognized that profit was a reward for assuming the risk of producing a product that the consumer wants to buy.

Table 5.5: Purpose of Profits[a]

Response	General Public (n=2,475)
Reward business for producing what consumers want[b]	41%
Pay for the wages and salaries of workers	34
Transfer income to the wealthy	16
Some/combination/all	5
Don't know/Refused	4

Notes:
[a]"Which of the following is the basic purpose of profits in our market economy?" [2]
[b]Correct response

The percentage of correct responses to the above five questions can be summed to create an average score to provide an estimate of entrepreneurial knowledge. It would, of course, be beneficial to have the results from more questions on such a test to provide a more reliable and valid estimate of the understanding of entrepreneurship among Nebraskans, but that was not possible given the survey constraints. The five questions do provide a sample of questions about entrepreneurship that could be asked of the respondents, and thus offer some insights about the general knowledge level of the subject.

The overall score was 63.4 percent correct. This score would rate only a "D" grade on a traditional "A" to "F" grading scale. Obviously, using such a grading scale is overly harsh in this case because the survey respondents were not taking a course and they were asked the questions without any prior study or warning. There also are various factors that contribute to the lowering of the score such as the level of education, age, and life experience. Nevertheless, the general conclusion that can be drawn from the results from these five questions is that there are substantial gaps in the entrepreneurial knowledge of the general public in Nebraska.

This conclusion is largely consistent with the opinions from the general public when asked to rate their level of entrepreneurial knowledge (Table 5.6). When asked to rate their knowledge and understanding of starting and managing a business, about six in ten (61%) placed themselves in the three lower categories of *fair* (31%), *poor* (17%), or *very poor* (13%) ratings. On the upside of the rating scale, about four in ten (39%) gave themselves either a *good* (23%) or *excellent* (16%) rating. These results also show that there is a lack of confidence among the general public in their entrepreneurial abilities that corresponds to the lack of knowledge as indicated by their responses to the three test questions.

Table 5.6: Knowledge of Starting and Managing a Business[a]

Response	General Public (n=4,935)	Business Owners Then (n=1,122)	Business Owners Now (n=567)
	%	%	%
5 Excellent	16	11	28
4 *(Good)*	23	25	43
3 *(Fair)*	31	35	22
2 *(Poor)*	17	20	3
1 Very poor	13	9	4
Don't know/Refused	1	0	0

Note: [a]For the General Public, the question was: "Using a five-point scale, where 5 is excellent and 1 is very poor, how would you describe your knowledge and understanding of starting and managing a business?" For Business Owners, the first question was: "Using a five-point scale, where 5 is excellent and 1 is very poor, how would you describe your knowledge and understanding of starting and managing a business, at the time you started your current business?" [3P; 3B(Then); 2B(Now)]

No one can be an expert in every area of knowledge, especially if it is one in which they have limited interest. Yet, the prior results show that many Nebraskans do have a strong interest in starting a business (see Table 4.1). If they are to achieve their goal and be successful, then it would be beneficial if they had more understanding of entrepreneurship. In addition, even those Nebraskans who are not interested in entrepreneurship or who are retired still have something at stake with entrepreneurship because it affects the economic growth of the state and the creation of jobs. Having a good understanding of entrepreneurship even among those who will never become entrepreneurs creates the climate of support for those who will undertake the entrepreneurial challenge.

It may be surprising that the responses of the small business owners in Nebraska were similar to those of the general public because it would be expected that small business owners would know more and be more confident about their knowledge and understanding of starting a business. There was, however, a difference in the way that their question was phrased which explains this similarity. In a first question, the small business owners were asked to rate their knowledge and understanding of starting and managing a business *at the time they started their current business* ("Then" column).

In a second question they were asked the same basic question, but were requested to supply an assessment based on their current knowledge ("Now" column). Obviously in retrospect, these small business owners realized that they had a lot to learn and that they were not as educated or well-prepared at the time they started their current businesses. Most business owners (71%) currently, however, consider their knowledge to be excellent (28%) or good (43%). These results re-emphasize the important role that work experience and education can play in better preparing for entrepreneurship in Nebraska.

A lack of entrepreneurial knowledge may adversely affect the climate for entrepreneurship in the state. Further indication to support this point comes from an opinion item on the survey (Table 5.7). To probe further to see how strong the support for competitive markets was among the general public in Nebraska, this question was asked: *Suppose a business in Nebraska raises the price of its product because the demand for it increased even though the cost of producing the product has not increased. Do you think the manufacturer should be allowed to raise prices?*

In this question, the rationale for the price increase came from increased demand by consumers for the product. There are many examples in a market economy of businesses raising prices based on increased demand. Hotels increase room rates and airlines raise ticket prices in peak tourist seasons. Car manufacturers raise prices (or offer fewer discounts) for popular models.

Gasoline prices rise because of increased demand during summer months which is a peak period for driving. The prices of stocks and bonds rise with increased demand. Allowing prices to change provides incentives for the efficient use and allocation of products and resources in a market economy.

Table 5.7: Business Wants to Raise Prices[a]

Response	General Public (n=2,475)
Yes, business should be allowed to raise prices	46%
No, not allowed to raise prices	50
Don't know/Refused	5

Note: [a]"Suppose a business in Nebraska raises the price of its product because the demand for it has increased even though the cost of manufacturing it has not increased. Do you think the manufacturer should be allowed to raise prices?" [2]

For this question, the opinion of Nebraskans was clearly split. The majority (50%) of the general public was opposed to the price increase and did not want the business to be allowed to raise prices. In this case, Nebraskans are not thinking like business owners who are operating in a world of supply and demand. Instead they were looking at this situation from their perspective as consumers and the adverse effect of higher prices on consumers. This perspective is not conducive to the development of an entrepreneurial climate in Nebraska, and in the extreme, such a perspective is likely to result in calls for government intervention into competitive markets and price regulation. Almost half (46%) of Nebraskans, however, were accepting of this price change and saw no reason to restrict the business from raising its price. There appears to be a sizable minority in the state who do have an economic mindset that is supportive of the price function in markets.

PREPARATION AND EDUCATION

Entrepreneurs are not just born to become entrepreneurs; they are subject to many influences and conditions that shape their thinking and prepare them for starting a business. The influences can include working at other businesses or learning from other entrepreneurs. Friends and family can also shape the thinking of future business owners. Education, both at the pre-college and college levels, can make a contribution to starting a business. These various influences and conditions that affect thinking are shown by the responses to a question asking about preparation for starting a business (Table 5.8).

Table 5.8: Valuable Preparation for Starting Current Business[a]

Response (% yes)	Business Owners (n=567)
Working at another business	83%
Learning from other entrepreneurs	78
Learning from friends or family	59
Participating in community activities	48
Learning about business and entrepreneurship in school or college	42

Note: [a]"Which of the following do you think gave you valuable preparation for starting your current business?" [2]

At the top of the list selected by small business owners is work experiences (83% say yes). Such an experience can be either positive or negative. It can be positive because the entrepreneur gains business skills and on-the-job training that can be carried over to the new business venture. It can be negative if the experience of working at another business was too restrictive, led to boredom or frustration, and did not meet the expectations of the aspiring entrepreneur. Such a work environment can help aspiring entrepreneurs recognize what they do not like and to create what they do like.

Almost as important as other work experience is learning from other entrepreneurs (78%). This learning can occur through mentoring, networking, or reading. Friends and family also are important (59%). In some cases, a parent or friend may have started their own business or has substantial business experience to share with a budding entrepreneur. It would be expected that entrepreneurs would value what is learned from the people closest to them. Participating in community activities (48%) was valuable too for about half of these small business owners. Such participation also fosters networking, opportunity recognition, and the development of leadership and multi-tasking business skills.

At the bottom of the list is formal education about business and entrepreneurship that is provided in schools or colleges (42%). Although the low percentage compared with the other factors may indicate that formal education is not important for the majority of entrepreneurs, this interpretation needs to be qualified. The question asked what gave small business owners valuable preparation. The responses with the highest ratings on the list are the ones that are also more current and immediate for small business owners to consider, such as working at another business or learning from other entrepreneurs. Formal education in school or college may have occurred in the distant past and therefore may not be thought to be as valuable. Some entrepreneurs may not have attended college and may not have received any business education in the high schools during the time period in which they went to high school. Given these conditions, the results indicate that for many small business entrepreneurs in Nebraska, this formal education had value.

A similar question probing for what helps entrepreneurs was asked in an open-ended format requesting that small business owners state just one factor that gave them the *most preparation* for starting a business (Table 5.9). The value of this open-ended probing is that the small business owner has to reply with the top response that comes to mind rather than select all the responses that apply from a list of choices. What emerges from the responses is a variety of factors, but they are not given the same weight as in the previous question.

Table 5.9: Most Preparation for Starting Business[a]

Response	Business Owners (n=555)	
	%	%
Life Experiences		27
Education and Skills		23
Education in school	13	
Talking with other entrepreneurs	4	
Ability to spot an opportunity and go with it	3	
Reading about starting a business	2	
Extracurricular or community activities	1	
Family		18
Learning from a family business	13	
Talking with family	5	
Working at Another Business		24
Other		1
Don't know/Refused		7

Note: [a]"What do you think gave you the most preparation for starting your current business?" [1]

The important role of education as preparation for entrepreneurship is now more clearly evident. About a quarter (23%) of small business owners in Nebraska thought informal or formal education gave them the most preparation for starting a business. This education was viewed as being of about equal importance to life experiences (27%) and the experience gained by working at another business (24%), and it was less important than family influences (18%).

Such factors as life experiences, family situation, or working at another business are important ones for shaping entrepreneurial thinking because they set the conditions under which a person lives and works, but they do not necessarily dominate the list.   In these cases, the preparation for entrepreneurship typically occurs in reaction to those conditions or situations – something happens in life, within a family, or on the job.   Education, however, is more of a pro-active factor because typically a decision is made to participate in it and the amount of it can be more easily changed to influence the degree of preparation a person has to become an entrepreneur. It may also be the one factor that can be more easily changed or subject to policy influence for a broader group.

Further probing of the preparation and education issue among Nebraska small business owners was conducted via a set of structured items asking about the importance of factors in making the decision to start a business (Table 5.10).   In this respect, the question was similar to the other closed-ended item (Table 5.8) in that it provided a menu of choices from which to pick, rather than asking the respondent to select the top choice, but in this case the survey question had a technology focus.

Table 5.10: Importance of Factors in Starting a Business[a]

| Response: **Business Owners** (n=555) | VI | | | | NI | |
	5	4	3	2	1	DK
	%	%	%	%	%	%
A. Work experience in the technology area	38	20	13	9	19	2
B. Education in or before high school	35	21	22	5	18	0
C. Education in a college or university	28	20	14	7	31	0
D. Using personal computers	22	20	14	7	37	0
E. Conversations with friends or family	15	21	26	15	23	1
F. Using the Internet and World Wide Web	15	14	12	13	46	0
G. Seeing something in the media	4	7	20	20	48	1

Note: [a]"Using a five-point scale, where 5 is very important (VI), and 1 is not at all important (NI), how important were the following factors in your decision to start a business?" [1]

The responses in the table are rank-ordered from highest to lowest based on summing the top two rating categories of *very important* (5) and *important* (4).   The item drawing the largest total of the very important or important responses (58%) was work experience in the technology area.   Also noteworthy in the technology area were using personal computers (42%) and using the Internet and World Wide Web (29%).

What is of equal or greater importance than the technology or job factors in the listing are the education factors. Education in high school or before high school (56%) was rated essentially the same as working in the technology area (58%) in terms of its importance. It was followed in turn by college or university education (48%). The likely reason that fewer business owners cited college or university education than high school education was because not all business owners went to a college or university. In addition, conversations with friends or family (36%) can be viewed as a form of informal education for prospective entrepreneurs. Taken together, the responses to these factors show that education is well-regarded by business owners in Nebraska as contributing to their decision to start a business.

The respect for education is shown in a follow-up question that was asked of those small business owners in Nebraska who attended a college or university. They were given a list of items about that education to evaluate the importance of its contribution to their starting a business (Table 5.11).

Table 5.11: Importance of Undergraduate Factors[a]

| Response: *Business Owners* (n=407)[b] | VI | | | | NI | |
	5	4	3	2	1	DK
	%	%	%	%	%	%
A. Classes that taught business or entrepreneurship	21	35	18	11	13	1
B. Classes that taught about technology	18	24	23	13	22	2
C. Classes that used technology	21	18	25	14	22	2
D. A key professor or professors	19	20	23	16	22	0
E. Extracurricular activities	12	18	25	17	28	0

Notes:
[a]"Using a five-point scale, where 5 is very important (VI), and 1 is not at all important (NI), how important were the following factors from your undergraduate education in your decision to start a business?" [1]
[b]Those who attended college as undergraduates.

At the top of the list of items rated as very important or important were classes that taught business or entrepreneurship (56%), as might be expected. Formal education does make a difference in the decision to start a business in the minds of Nebraska small business owners. This item was followed in the ratings by classes that taught about technology (42%), classes that used technology (39%), and a key professor or professors (39%). Extracurricular activities (30%) were viewed as being the least important to the entrepreneurship decision.

Although much attention is often focused on the undergraduate level as a basis for entrepreneurship, the fact is that entrepreneurial thinking begins at a much earlier age and it affects a wider range of the population than those who attend a college or university. That understanding is shown in the responses of the small business owners in Nebraska, over half (56%) of whom gave a high school education such a high rating of importance compared with all other factors (see Table 5.10). An additional question was also asked of small business owners to probe for what within a high school education seemed to be influential in the decision to start a business (Table 5.12).

Table 5.12: Importance of High School Education[a]

Response: *Business Owners* (n=555)	VI 5	4	3	2	NI 1	DK
	%	%	%	%	%	%
A. A key teacher or teachers	24	20	21	13	22	0
B. Classes that taught business or entrepreneurship	21	19	24	10	26	0
C. Classes that used technology	18	17	24	7	35	0
D. Extracurricular activities	14	17	31	13	24	1
E. Classes that taught about technology	15	15	22	13	35	1

Note: [a]"Using a five-point scale, where 5 is very important (VI), and 1 is not at all important (NI), how important were the following factors from your high school education in your decision to start a business?" [1]

The list of factors was about the same as those given for the college or university question. The responses in the table are rank-ordered from top to bottom based on summing the *very important* and *important* responses. What goes to the top of this list is the role of a key teacher or teachers (44%). The role of the teacher is closely followed by the influence of classes that taught business or entrepreneurship (40%). The results suggest that the value of a high school education for entrepreneurship can be enhanced if students have more exposure to classes that teach about business and entrepreneurship, and if they have teachers who recognize and encourage entrepreneurial inclinations. The personal influence from key teachers, regardless of the subjects taught, is especially valuable as they have the potential to shape the decisions of future entrepreneurs in the state. If more teachers understood the contribution they can make to entrepreneurship in the state, more of this potential would be realized.

The value of high school education for entrepreneurship is recognized by the general public. When asked how important it was that the schools teach students about entrepreneurship and starting a business (Table 5.13), five in ten (51%) stated that it was *very important* and another almost three in ten (29%) stated it was *important*. The combined total of eight in ten (80%) showed that the general public in Nebraska understands and appreciates what entrepreneurship education can do for youth.

Table 5.13: Importance of Schools to Teach about Entrepreneurship[a]

Response	General Public (n=4,935)	Business Owners (n=567)
	%	%
5 Very important	51	65
4	29	21
3	15	11
2	3	2
1 Not at all important	2	2
Don't know/Refused	1	0

Note: [a]"Using a five-point scale, where 5 is very important, and 1 is not at all important, how important is it for our nation's schools to teach students about entrepreneurship and starting a business?" [3P, 2B]

The reasons for this strong recommendation are worth considering. The results from the first table (Table 4.1) showed that many Nebraskans, especially young adults, want to start a business. Given this level of entrepreneurial interest, it should not be surprising that most of the general public thought it was important for the schools to teach more about entrepreneurship and starting a business. Contributing to this strong support for more entrepreneurship education are probably some negative factors. The general public in Nebraska showed deficiencies in entrepreneurial knowledge (Tables 5.1–5.5) and recognized its lack of the necessary knowledge and understanding for starting a business (Table 5.6). In addition, bad experience in the job market or limited incomes may lend support to the importance of entrepreneurship because it is viewed as a way for the youth in the state to avoid such problems when they become adults. Whatever the reasons, the basic recommendation that emerges from the general public in Nebraska is the need for more education in entrepreneurship in the schools.

Small business owners in Nebraska are even more emphatic in their responses than the general public. Almost two-thirds (65%) stated that it is *very important* that schools teach students about entrepreneurship and starting a business and more than two in ten (21%) stated that it was *important*. The combined total is almost nine in ten (86%) and indicates that there is overwhelming support among small business owners for entrepreneurship education in the schools. The responses also provide further indication that small business owners see a great deal of value in entrepreneurship for the state and would like to encourage it.

Another way to assess the view of the general public and small business owners in Nebraska on this issue is to ask whether they think that if schools focus more on entrepreneurship education, it would probably result in more entrepreneurship in the state (Table 5.14). The support for such a proposition is less overwhelming than was the case with the previous question that asked for a general rating of the importance of entrepreneurship education, in part because the current question requires an evaluation of the direct connection between entrepreneurship education in schools and an increase in entrepreneurship in the state. Nevertheless, a sizable majority of the general public (57%) and small business owners (60%) either strongly agree or agree with the proposition and support the connection between pre-college entrepreneurship education and its effect on the eventual number of entrepreneurs in the state.

Table 5.14: Schools Should Focus More on Entrepreneurship Education[a]

Response	General Public (n=2,475)	Business Owners (n=567)
	%	%
5 Strongly agree	31	30
4	26	30
3	28	26
2	8	10
1 Strongly disagree	5	4
Don't know/Refused	2	1

Note: [a]"Using a five-point scale, where 5 is strongly agree, and 1 is strongly disagree, please indicate if you agree or disagree with the following statement: If our schools focused more on entrepreneurship education, more people would probably start their own businesses." [2]

The same two questions can also be asked about the value of college education. The importance of education for entrepreneurship at this level is recognized by the general public and small business owners in Nebraska (Table 5.15). Almost six in ten (58%) of the general public and almost seven in ten (68%) of small business owners stated that it is *very important.* Over a quarter (27%) of the general public and two in ten (20%) of small business owners also stated that it was *important.* Taken together, the great majority of both groups see significant value in entrepreneurship education in colleges and universities.

Table 5.15: Importance of Colleges to Teach about Entrepreneurship[a]

Response	General Public (n=2,475)	Business Owners (n=567)
	%	%
5 Very important	58	68
4	27	20
3	12	8
2	2	1
1 Not at all important	1	2
Don't know/Refused	1	–

Note: [a]"Using a five-point scale, where 5 is very important, and 1 is not at all important, how important is it for our nation's colleges and universities to teach students about entrepreneurship and starting a business?" [2]

The high degree of support for entrepreneurship education in colleges and universities also is displayed in responses to the question that asks the general public and small business owners in Nebraska to assess the connection between such education and business start-ups in the state (Table 5.16). Both groups see the connection and also accept this general conclusion in about the same proportion and with a similar response to what they stated in reply to the school version of the question. More than six in ten of the general public (62%) and small business owners (66%) in Nebraska either strongly agree or agree with the proposition that there is a connection between collegiate education in entrepreneurship and its effect on the number of people who will start a business. Only slightly more than one in ten in each group either disagree or strongly disagree with the proposition.

Table 5.16: Colleges Should Focus More on Entrepreneurship Education[a]

Response	General Public (n=2,475)	Business Owners (n=567)
	%	%
5 Strongly agree	33	35
4	29	31
3	24	22
2	7	8
1 Strongly disagree	5	5
Don't know/Refused	1	–

Note: [a]"Using a five-point scale, where 5 is strongly agree, and 1 is strongly disagree, please indicate if you agree or disagree with the following statement: If our colleges and universities focused more on entrepreneurship education, more people would probably start their own businesses." [2]

COMPARISONS: COMMUNITY COLLEGE REGIONS, BUSINESS SIZES, AND NATIONAL

In the previous chapter, the results showed that there was minimal variation in the survey responses when they were compared across community college regions or districts in Nebraska (see Figure 2.4 for a district map). That general conclusion also applies to the survey items discussed in the current chapter, which are supplied in Appendix 5A.

To illustrate this point, consider the results for the knowledge questions and the self-ratings of knowledge. The correct responses to the five knowledge questions can be aggregated into a mean score for the general public overall and by community college district (Tables 5.1a–5.5a). The mean score for the state is 63.4 percent correct. It ranges from 59 percent correct to 67 percent correct by community college district: Metropolitan (67); Southeast (62); Central (62), Northeast (59), Mid-Plains (62), and Western (62). The eight-point difference in the range of scores is relatively small and within the margin of sampling error for community college regions. In addition, the self-ratings of knowledge and understanding of starting a business showed that less than half of the general public in each region would give themselves either an excellent or good rating. The ratings ranged from a low of 36% for excellent and good combined to a high of 44% across the regions (Table 5.6a), which again is within the margin of sampling error for the region data.

When education factors are considered, the differences of opinion across regions is again relatively limited. For example, from 78 to 84 percent of the general public in each community college district think that it is *very important* or *important* for schools to teach about entrepreneurship and starting a business (Table 5.13a). When a similar question is asked about the undergraduate education, from 81 to 87 percent the general public in each district think that it is *very important* or *important* for colleges to teach about entrepreneurship and starting a business (Table 5.15a).

The differences in question responses among the small business owners by the size of the firm are reported in Appendix 5B. Two items that show the most sizable differences are the self-ratings of knowledge of starting and managing a business, both at the time the current business was started (Table 5.6b_1) and now (Table 5.6b_2). A greater percentage of business owners with one to ten employees said that their knowledge was *excellent* or *good* when they started their current business than did business owners of other size firms (37% versus 28–29%). By contrast, a smaller percentage of business owners with one to ten employees stated that their knowledge of starting and managing business now was excellent or good compared with larger-sized firms (73% versus 83–88%). Also noteworthy is the fact that business owners of the largest firms, those with 50 to 100 employees, gave themselves the highest self-rating of their knowledge of starting and managing a firm (88%), perhaps because of the greater complexity involved with larger businesses especially compared with the smallest ones.

In terms of their preparation, the views of small business owners by firm size are quite similar. For example, they give about the same rank ordering in their responses to items considered to be valuable preparation for starting their current business (Table 5.8b). At the top of the list is working at another business or learning from other entrepreneurs, each with about eight in ten (78% to 84%) business owners saying it was valuable. At the bottom of the list was participating in community activities or learning about business and entrepreneurship in school or college, with only about four to five in ten (38% to 49%) saying they were valuable. In between the two extremes was learning from friends or family, with about six in ten (56% to 60%) supplying that response.

Also indicative of the similarity in views on preparation are the responses given to an open-ended question about the most preparation (Table 5.9b). About the same percentages in each group supplied answers that attributed most preparation to life experiences (22–27%), education and skills (20–25%), and family (15–20%). Also receiving a strong rating was working at another business, but there was more variation in response by firm size. Over a third (34–35%) of business owners of firms with 11 or more employees cite working at another business as giving them the most preparation for starting a business, but less than a quarter (23%) of business owners of firms with one to ten employees thought it gave them the most preparation.

That small business owners with one to ten employees are somewhat different from other business owners is suggested by responses to other questions about work or education. Owners of the smallest firms are more likely to cite something related to technology as being very important than is the case for the other business owners. The differences can be seen in responses about work in the technology area (Table 5.10b: 39% versus 26–30%), college classes that taught about technology (Table 5.11b: 19% versus 9–12%); college classes that used technology (Table 5.11b: 21% versus 12–14%); high school classes that used technology (Table 5.12b: 19% versus 8–10%); and high school classes that taught about technology (15% versus 5–10%).

In terms of the importance for teaching about entrepreneurship in schools or college, there is substantial agreement and a high degree of support across the business owner groups. From 82 to 90 percent think it is either *very important* or *important* for schools to teach about entrepreneurship and starting a business (Table 5.13b). An even higher level of support (85–93%) is given to the proposition that it is very important or important for colleges to teach about entrepreneurship (Table 5.15b).

The results for each of the five knowledge question are supplied in the first five tables of Appendix 5C. Calculation of the mean score for a national sample of the general public in the United States produces a mean score of 63.6 percent correct, which is essentially the same as the 63.4 percent correct for the general public in Nebraska. The results indicate that the general public in Nebraska exhibits the same relatively low level of entrepreneurial knowledge as does the general public nationwide. Both the state and national samples of the general public also give themselves similar relatively low ratings on their entrepreneurial knowledge (61% to fair to very poor for Nebraskans and 65% fair to very poor nationwide) (Table 5.6c).

The only other item for which there are state and national results is the on the importance of having the nation's schools teach about entrepreneurship and starting a business (Table 5.13c). Adding the *very important* and *important* responses together for the state and national samples shows remarkable similarity in both samples. This similarity in the importance rating is found both with state and national samples of the general public (80–81%) and also for small business owners (86–88%).

CONCLUSION

The climate for entrepreneurship in Nebraska can be affected by the level of entrepreneurial knowledge people possess and the education or preparation for entrepreneurship that people receive before they undertake new venture creation. More entrepreneurial knowledge and education means that there will be more human capital for entrepreneurship and greater support for it in the state. Both the knowledge and education factors were investigated in this chapter and the survey analysis produces the following findings.

- Nebraskans have only a limited knowledge and understanding of entrepreneurship, but they are aware of their deficiencies. The level of basic knowledge in the state is about the same as it is nationally.
- There are many influences that give people preparation for starting a business; the most important ones include life experiences, working at another business, family effects, and education.

- Education, at both the high school and college and university levels, makes a prime contribution to the decision to start a business according to small business owners in Nebraska. Business owners of firms with the smallest number of employees appear to highly value their technology-based education as preparation for entrepreneurship.
- Only minor differences are found in the level of entrepreneurial knowledge and education for entrepreneurship among the general public across the state by community college district.
- Both the general public and small business owners in Nebraska highly recommend that schools, and colleges and universities, should teach students more about entrepreneurship and starting a business.

This final point needs to be given some extra attention. There is widespread support and agreement among the general public and small business owners in Nebraska that pre-college and college education in entrepreneurship is important. A large majority of both groups think that if schools and colleges gave more focus to entrepreneurship education at their respective levels, such actions would contribute to entrepreneurial initiatives in the state. The recognition of the importance of entrepreneurship education by both groups could serve as a basis for expansion of entrepreneurship in Nebraska.

NOTES

1. At the end of each question for each table is a code in square brackets: The [1] refers to items given only in the 2005 survey. The code [2] refers to items given only in the 2006 survey. The code [3] refers to a survey given both years. If a survey was given to one group but not another in a particular year, the code includes a symbol for either the general public (P) or small business owners (B) to indicate that group distinction for a survey item.

APPENDIX 5A: General Public by Community College

Table 5.1a: Description of Entrepreneur[a] (n=2,460)

	Community College District					
	Metro- politan	South- east	Central	North- east	Mid- Plains	Western
Response	(n=419)	(399)	(408)	(412)	(404)	(419)
	%	%	%	%	%	%
A person who starts a business[b]	94	92	88	87	91	90
A manager of a large corporation	4	4	6	8	5	7
A government official running a regulatory agency	1	2	2	2	1	1
Some/combination/all	0	1	1	0	0	0
Don't know/Refused	1	2	3	2	2	2

Notes:
[a]"Which of the following best describes an entrepreneur?" [1]
[b]Correct response

Table 5.2a: Who Created Most New Jobs in Past Ten Years[a] (n=2,460)

	Community College District					
	Metro- politan	South- east	Central	North- east	Mid- Plains	Western
Response	(n=420)	(398)	(407)	(412)	(405)	(420)
	%	%	%	%	%	%
Small businesses[b]	51	52	49	46	44	44
Large businesses	36	36	39	38	37	39
The Federal government	11	8	8	12	14	13
Some/combination/all	0	1	1	1	0	1
None	0	1	1	1	1	0
Don't know/Refused	2	3	3	2	4	3

Notes:
[a]"Over the last ten years, which of the following groups has created the most new jobs in the economy?" [1]
[b]Correct response

Table 5.3a: Most Important Factor for Business Survival[a] (n=4,935)

Response	Community College District					
	Metro-politan (n=819)	South-east (801)	Central (807)	North-east (827)	Mid-Plains (858)	Western (823)
	%	%	%	%	%	%
The company's cash flow[b]	69	64	70	65	70	68
The value of the company's common stock	11	11	10	11	9	11
Having a board of directors	6	7	5	6	5	6
Having a low depreciation rate	6	11	8	9	8	8
Some/combination/all	3	2	2	2	3	2
Don't know/Refused	4	5	5	7	6	5

Notes:
[a]"Over the last ten years, which of the following groups has created the most new jobs in the economy?" [1]
[b]Correct response

Table 5.4a: Determination of Prices[a] (n=2,475)

Response	Community College District					
	Metro-politan (n=400)	South-east (402)	Central (400)	North-east (415)	Mid-Plains (454)	Western (404)
	%	%	%	%	%	%
Supply and demand for products[b]	73	62	68	60	66	71
Local, state, or Federal government	7	9	11	11	10	6
The Consumer Price Index	7	13	9	10	9	9
Monetary policy of the Federal Reserve	5	5	3	4	3	3
Some/combination/all	5	4	2	5	6	3
None	1	0	0	1	0	1
Don't know/Refused	3	7	7	9	6	7

Notes:
[a]"To the best of your knowledge, the prices of most products in a competitive market, like the United States, are determined by?" [2]
[b]Correct response

Table 5.5a: Purpose of Profits[a] (n=2,475)

	Community College District					
Response	Metro-politan (n=400)	South-east (402)	Central (400)	North-east (415)	Mid-Plains (454)	Western (404)
	%	%	%	%	%	%
Reward businesses for producing what consumers want[b]	47	39	37	38	39	38
Pay for the wages and salaries of workers	29	33	42	41	35	36
Transfer income to the wealthy	17	17	16	12	16	16
Some/combination/all	4	4	2	3	5	4
None	1	1	1	1	1	1
Don't know/Refused	3	5	4	5	5	6

Notes:
[a]"Which of the following is the basic purpose of profits in our market economy?" [2]
[b]Correct response

Table 5.6a: Knowledge of Starting and Managing a Business[a] (n=4,935)

	Community College District					
Response	Metro-politan (n=819)	South-east (801)	Central (807)	North-east (827)	Mid-Plains (858)	Western (823)
	%	%	%	%	%	%
5 Excellent	16	15	15	17	16	16
4	21	23	21	27	26	28
3	31	30	32	29	28	28
2	18	19	17	15	14	14
1 Very poor	13	13	14	11	15	13
Don't know/Refused	1	1	1	1	1	1

Note: [a]"Using a five-point scale, where 5 is excellent and 1 is very poor, how would you describe your knowledge and understanding of starting and managing a business?" [2]

Table 5.7a: *Business Wants to Raise Prices*[a] (n=2,475)

Response	Community College District					
	Metro-politan (n=400)	South-east (402)	Central (400)	North-east (415)	Mid-Plains (454)	Western (404)
	%	%	%	%	%	%
Yes, allowed to	47	50	41	40	41	44
No, not allowed to	48	46	55	55	55	52
Don't know/Refused	5	4	4	5	2	4

Note: [a]"Suppose a business in Nebraska raises the price of its product because the demand for it has increased even though the cost of manufacturing it has not increased. Do you think the manufacturer should be allowed to raise prices?" [2]

Table 5.13a: *Importance of Schools to Teach about Entrepreneurship*[a] (n=4,935)

Response	Community College District					
	Metro-politan (n=819)	South-east (801)	Central (807)	North-east (827)	Mid-Plains (858)	Western (823)
	%	%	%	%	%	%
5 Very important	50	51	54	51	51	54
4	28	30	29	32	32	30
3	17	13	15	13	12	12
2	3	4	2	1	3	2
1 Not at all important	2	2	1	2	1	2
Don't know/Refused	0	1	0	1	1	0

Note: [a]"Using a five-point scale, where 5 is very important, and 1 is not at all important, how important is it for our nation's schools to teach students about entrepreneurship and starting a business?" [3]

Table 5.14a: Schools Should Focus More on Entrepreneurship Education[a] (n=2,475)

	Community College District					
	Metro-politan	South-east	Central	North-east	Mid-Plains	Western
Response	(n=400)	(402)	(400)	(415)	(454)	(404)
	%	%	%	%	%	%
5 Strongly agree	32	30	28	35	30	33
4	26	23	31	26	27	25
3	29	29	27	24	28	29
2	7	9	7	7	8	6
1 Strongly disagree	4	7	5	5	5	6
Don't know/Refused	1	2	3	3	2	1

Note: [a]"Using a five-point scale, where 5 is strongly agree, and 1 is strongly disagree, please indicate if you agree or disagree with the following statement: If our schools focused more on entrepreneurship education, more people would probably start their own businesses." [2]

Table 5.15a: Importance of Colleges to Teach about Entrepreneurship[a] (n=2,475)

	Community College District					
	Metro-politan	South-east	Central	North-east	Mid-Plains	Western
Response	(n=400)	(402)	(400)	(415)	(454)	(404)
	%	%	%	%	%	%
5 Very important	53	62	60	57	57	64
4	28	23	26	30	30	23
3	16	11	11	8	9	9
2	2	2	1	2	1	2
1 Not at all important	1	3	1	1	2	1
Don't know/Refused	0	1	1	2	2	1

Note: [a]"Using a five-point scale, where 5 is very important, and 1 is not at all important, how important is it for our nation's colleges and universities to teach students about entrepreneurship and starting a business?" [2]

Table 5.16a: Colleges Should Focus More on Entrepreneurship Education[a] (n=2,475)

| Response | Community College District | | | | | |
	Metro-politan (n=400)	South-east (402)	Central (400)	North-east (415)	Mid-Plains (454)	Western (404)
	%	%	%	%	%	%
5 Strongly agree	32	33	34	35	33	39
4	33	25	32	27	29	25
3	25	24	20	25	25	24
2	6	9	7	6	7	7
1 Strongly disagree	4	7	5	4	4	5
Don't know/Refused	1	2	2	3	2	1

Note: [a]"Using a five-point scale, where 5 is strongly agree, and 1 is strongly disagree, please indicate if you agree or disagree with the following statement: If our colleges and universities focused more on entrepreneurship education, more people would probably start their own businesses." [2]

APPENDIX 5B: Business Owners by Number of Employees

Table 5.6b_1:   Knowledge of Starting and Managing a Business (Then)[a] (n=1,122)

	Number of Employees			
	1–10	**11–19**	**20–49**	**50–100**
Response	(n=322)	(314)	(296)	(190)
	%	%	%	%
5 Excellent	12 ·	8	10	9
4	25	20	19	20
3	35	39	36	48
2	19	24	25	16
1 Very poor	9	9	9	6

Note: [a]"Using a five-point scale, where 5 is excellent and 1 is very poor, how would you describe your knowledge and understanding of starting and managing a business, *at the time you started your current business?*" [3]

Table 5.6b_2:   Knowledge of Starting and Managing a Business (Now)[a] (n=567)

	Number of Employees			
	1–10	**11–19**	**20–49**	**50–100**
Response	(n=172)	(162)	(146)	(87)
	%	%	%	%
5 Excellent	30	31	41	36
4	43	52	42	52
3	20	14	14	8
2	3	2	2	5
1 Very poor	4	2	1	0

Note: [a]"Using a five-point scale, where 5 is excellent and 1 is very poor, how would you describe your knowledge and understanding of starting and managing a business?" [2]

Table 5.8b: Valuable Preparation for Starting Current Business[a] (n=567)

Response	Yes	No
	%	%
A. Working at another business		
1–10 employees (n=172)	83	17
11–19 employees (n=162)	78	22
20–49 employees (n=146)	80	20
50–100 employees (n=87)	82	18
B. Learning from other entrepreneurs		
1–10 employees	79	22
11–19 employees	84	16
20–49 employees	79	21
50–100 employees	86	14
C. Learning from friends or family		
1–10 employees	60	40
11–19 employees	59	41
20–49 employees	56	44
50–100 employees	58	43
D. Participating in community activities		
1–10 employees	48	52
11–19 employees	41	59
20–49 employees	38	62
50–100 employees	47	53
E. Learning about business and entrepreneurship in school or college		
1–10 employees	43	57
11–19 employees	44	56
20–49 employees	39	61
50–100 employees	49	51

Note: [a]"Which of the following do you think gave you valuable preparation for starting your current business?" [2]

Table 5.9b: Most Preparation for Starting Business[a] *(n=555)*

Response	Number of Employees			
	1–10	**11–19**	**20–49**	**50–100**
	(n=150)	(152)	(179)	(74)
	%	%	%	%
Life Experiences	27	24	22	22
Education and Skills	23	20	25	25
Education in school	13	13	17	20
Talking with other entrepreneurs	4	1	3	4
Ability to spot an opportunity and go with it	3	2	2	1
Reading about starting a business	2	1	1	0
Extracurricular or community activities	1	3	2	0
Family	18	20	15	16
Learning from a family business	13	13	9	11
Talking with family	5	7	6	5
Working at Another Business	23	34	35	34
Other	1	1	0	0
Don't know/Refused	7	3	4	3

Note: [a]"What do you think gave you the most preparation for starting your current business?"
[1]

Table 5.10b: Importance of Factors in Starting a Business[a] (n=555)

Response	VI 5	4	3	2	NI 1	DK
	%	%	%	%	%	%
A. Work experience in the technology area						
1–10 employees (n=172)	39	19	12	9	19	2
11–19 employees (n=162)	26	21	22	12	19	0
20–49 employees (n=146)	30	24	18	12	16	0
50–100 employees (n=87)	26	15	19	8	30	3
B. Education in high school or before high school						
1–10 employees	35	21	22	4	19	0
11–19 employees	39	21	15	11	15	0
20–49 employees	31	22	20	9	17	1
50–100 employees	37	16	22	14	11	1
C. Education in a college or university						
1–10 employees	28	19	14	7	32	0
11–19 employees	29	23	16	9	23	0
20–49 employees	29	29	18	11	12	1
50–100 employees	30	24	16	10	19	1
D. Using personal computers						
1–10 employees	23	20	14	6	37	0
11–19 employees	20	15	17	11	38	0
20–49 employees	17	23	15	13	31	1
50–100 employees	20	10	18	10	39	4
E. Conversations with friends or family						
1–10 employees	15	21	26	15	22	1
11–19 employees	10	20	18	20	32	1
20–49 employees	13	18	27	16	26	0
50–100 employees	10	11	22	15	42	1
F. Using the Internet and World Wide Web						
1–10 employees	15	14	12	13	46	0
11–19 employees	7	11	17	14	52	0
20–49 employees	8	16	15	16	45	1
50–100 employees	12	4	20	11	50	3
G. Seeing something in the media						
1–10 employees	4	7	20	20	49	1
11–19 employees	7	9	18	21	45	0
20–49 employees	4	10	25	23	39	0
50–100 employees	4	7	26	20	42	1

Note: [a]"Using a five-point scale, where 5 is very important (VI), and 1 is not at all important (NI), how important were the following factors in your decision to start a business?" [1]

Table 5.11b: Importance of Undergraduate Factors[a] (n=407)[b]

Response	VI 5	4	3	2	NI 1
	%	%	%	%	%
A. Classes that taught business or entrepreneurship					
1–10 employees (n=98)	20	37	18	11	12
11–19 employees (n=110)	24	19	19	10	28
20–49 employees (n=140)	29	27	19	7	18
50–100 employees (n=59)	25	37	10	9	17
B. Classes that taught about technology					
1–10 employees	19	25	22	12	20
11–19 employees	10	14	18	20	37
20–49 employees	9	20	29	11	30
50–100 employees	12	22	24	10	31
C. Classes that used technology					
1–10 employees	21	17	26	14	20
11–19 employees	12	17	17	17	36
20–49 employees	14	24	21	14	27
50–100 employees	14	19	25	10	31
D. A key professor or professors					
1–10 employees	19	19	24	17	21
11–19 employees	17	17	14	15	37
20–49 employees	14	23	28	15	20
50–100 employees	19	25	20	12	22
E. Extracurricular activities					
1–10 employees	12	18	25	17	28
11–19 employees	12	16	25	13	36
20–49 employees	11	16	26	21	25
50–100 employees	17	7	32	10	32

Notes:
[a]"Using a five-point scale, where 5 is very important (VI), and 1 is not at all important (NI), how important were the following factors in your decision to start a business?" [1]
[b]Those who attended college as an undergraduate.

Table 5.12b: Importance of High School Education[a] (n=555)

Response	VI 5	4	3	2	NI 1
	%	%	%	%	%
A. A key teacher or teachers					
1–10 employees (n=150)	25	19	21	13	22
11–19 employees (n=152)	19	28	14	11	29
20–49 employees (n=179)	18	26	27	12	16
50–100 employees (n=74)	26	19	16	12	26
B. Classes that taught business or entrepreneurship					
1–10 employees	21	19	24	10	26
11–19 employees	20	19	20	9	32
20–49 employees	22	24	17	11	24
50–100 employees	18	23	22	8	28
C. Classes that used technology					
1–10 employees	19	17	24	6	35
11–19 employees	8	22	14	18	37
20–49 employees	10	18	25	14	32
50–100 employees	10	14	19	18	39
D. Extracurricular activities					
1–10 employees	14	17	31	13	24
11–19 employees	16	21	26	12	24
20–49 employees	11	26	24	16	22
50–100 employees	19	22	22	11	26
E. Classes that taught about technology					
1–10 employees	15	15	22	12	35
11–19 employees	10	16	16	22	35
20–49 employees	12	18	21	15	33
50–100 employees	5	11	28	12	42

Note: [a]"Using a five-point scale, where 5 is very important (VI), and 1 is not at all important (NI), how important were the following factors from your high school education in your decision to start a business?" [1]

Table 5.13b: Importance of Schools to Teach about Entrepreneurship[a]
(n=567)

Response	Number of Employees			
	1–10 (n=172)	**11–19** (162)	**20–49** (146)	**50–100** (87)
	%	**%**	**%**	**%**
5 Very important	64	61	53	64
4	23	21	30	26
3	10	12	10	7
2	2	3	3	2
1 Not at all important	2	2	4	0
Don't know/Refused	0	1	0	0

Note: [a]"Using a five-point scale, where 5 is very important, and 1 is not at all important, how important is it for our nation's schools to teach students about entrepreneurship and starting a business?" [2]

Table 5.14b: Schools Should Focus More on Entrepreneurship Education[a]
(n=567)

Response	Number of Employees			
	1–10 (n=172)	**11–19** (162)	**20–49** (146)	**50–100** (87)
	%	**%**	**%**	**%**
5 Strongly agree	31	32	30	39
4	31	25	31	37
3	25	30	27	16
2	9	7	7	6
1 Strongly disagree	4	6	6	2
Don't know/Refused	1	1	0	0

Note: [a]"Using a five-point scale, where 5 is strongly agree, and 1 is strongly disagree, please indicate if you agree or disagree with the following statement: If our schools focused more on entrepreneurship education, more people would probably start their own businesses." [2]

Table 5.15b: *Importance of Colleges to Teach about Entrepreneurship*[a] (Business Owners only; n=567)

Response	Number of Employees			
	1–10 (n=172)	11–19 (162)	20–49 (146)	50–100 (87)
	%	%	%	%
5 Very important	69	64	62	68
4	20	24	23	25
3	8	9	9	6
2	1	1	3	1
1 Not at all important	2	1	3	0

Note: [a]"Using a five-point scale, where 5 is very important, and 1 is not at all important, how important is it for our nation's colleges and universities to teach students about entrepreneurship and starting a business?" [2]

Table 5.16b: *Colleges Should Focus More on Entrepreneurship Education*[a] (n=567)

Response	Number of Employees			
	1–10 (n=172)	11–19 (162)	20–49 (146)	50–100 (87)
	%	%	%	%
5 Strongly agree	35	38	34	37
4	32	30	32	36
3	22	23	23	23
2	7	6	8	2
1 Strongly disagree	4	4	4	2

Note: [a]"Using a five-point scale, where 5 is strongly agree, and 1 is strongly disagree, please indicate if you agree or disagree with the following statement: If our colleges and universities focused more on entrepreneurship education, more people would probably start their own businesses." [2]

APPENDIX 5C: Nebraska vs. United States Data

Table 5.1c: Description of Entrepreneur[a]

Response	Nebraska (n=2,460)	U.S. (n=607)
	%	%
A person who starts a business[b]	91	85
A manager of a large corporation	5	9
A government official running a regulatory agency	1	3
Some/combination/all	1	1
Don't know/Refused	2	2

Notes:
[a]"Which of the following best describes an entrepreneur?" [1]
[b]Correct response

Table 5.2c: Who Created Most New Jobs in Past Ten Years[a]

Response	Nebraska (n=2,460)	U.S. (n=607)
	%	%
Small businesses[b]	50	55
Large businesses	37	27
The Federal government	10	13
Don't know/Refused	3	5

Notes:
[a]"Over the last ten years, which of the following groups has created the most new jobs in the economy?" [1]
[b]Correct response

Table 5.3c: Most Important Factor for Business Survival[a]

Response	Nebraska (n=4,395)	U.S. (n=607)
	%	%
The company's cash flow[b]	68	66
The value of the company's common stock	11	15
Having a board of directors	6	6
Having a low depreciation rate	9	8
Some/combination/all	3	1
Don't know/Refused	5	4

Notes:
[a]"Which factor is most important for business survival?" [3]
[b]Correct response

Table 5.4c: Determination of Prices[a]

Response	Nebraska (n=2,475)	U.S. (n=607)
	%	%
Supply and demand for products[b]	67	71
Local, state, or Federal government	9	8
The Consumer Price Index	9	12
Monetary policy of the Federal Reserve	4	4
Some/combination/all	5	1
Don't know/Refused	6	4

Notes:
[a]"To the best of your knowledge, the prices of most products in a competitive market, like the United States, are determined by?" [2]
[b]Correct response

Table 5.5c: Purpose of Profits[a]

Response	Nebraska (n=2475)	U.S. (n=607)
	%	%
Reward business for producing what consumers want[b]	41	41
Pay for the wages and salaries of workers	34	36
Transfer income to the wealthy	16	17
Some/combination/all	5	2
Don't know/Refused	4	4

Notes:
[a]"Which of the following is the basic purpose of profits in our market economy?" [2]
[b]Correct response

Table 5.6c: Knowledge of Starting and Managing a Business[a]

	General Public		Business Owners	
	Nebr.	U.S.	Nebr.	U.S.
Response	(n=4,935)	(607)	(1,122)	(403)
	%	%	%	%
5 Excellent	16	15	11	13
4	23	19	25	16
3	31	34	35	34
2	17	16	20	21
1 Very poor	13	15	9	16
Don't know/Refused	1	–	–	–

Note: [a]For the General Public, the question was: "Using a five-point scale, where 5 is excellent and 1 is very poor, how would you describe your knowledge and understanding of starting and managing a business?" For Business Owners, the first question was: "Using a five-point scale, where 5 is excellent and 1 is very poor, how would you describe your knowledge and understanding of starting and managing a business, at the time you started your current business?" [3]

Table 5.13c: Importance of Schools to Teach about Entrepreneurship[a]

	General Public		Business Owners	
	Nebr.	U.S.	Nebr.	U.S.
Response	(n=4,935)	(607)	(567)	(403)
	%	%	%	%
5 Very important	51	59	65	73
4	29	22	21	15
3	15	14	11	7
2	3	2	2	2
1 Not at all important	2	3	2	2
Don't know/Refused	1	–	0	1

Note: [a]"Using a five-point scale, where 5 is very important, and 1 is not at all important, how important is it for our nation's schools to teach students about entrepreneurship and starting a business?" [3P; 2B]

CHAPTER 6

Views of Government, Business, and Economic Development

The climate for entrepreneurship in Nebraska is shaped by many forces, one the most important of which is the Nebraska economy. Economic and business conditions can influence the willingness to assume the risk of starting new businesses and may determine whether they succeed or fail. The Nebraska economy, however, is a mixed one, which means that there is activity in both the public and private sectors that affect entrepreneurship.

In the public sector, government can direct the allocation of economic resources and affect new business formation in the state through its regulation and taxation powers. Government actions also can encourage or discourage economic development in communities across the state through the level and quality of the technical assistance or support for new projects that bring many economic benefits. In the private sector, business owners continually make decisions on a wide set of issues such as those involving financing, health care, workforce quality, or business succession. These private decisions directly or indirectly influence not only the success of particular businesses, but also economic development in communities throughout the state.

This chapter continues and completes the survey study of the climate for entrepreneurship in Nebraska by investigating the views of the general public and small business owners about the public and private sectors. The first part of the chapter provides opinions about the role of government in the economy. The second looks at general views of business. The third part discusses business issues and economic development.

THE ROLE OF GOVERNMENT

Government has valuable and legitimate functions in the Nebraska economy, but many of its actions may encourage or discourage entrepreneurship. Regulation of business is one of these functions of government. In this regard, the opinions of small business owners in Nebraska are relatively negative (Table 6.1). Seven in ten (70%) Nebraska small business owners thought there was too much government regulation of business and very few (4%) stated there was too little. This generally negative view of regulation among most small business owners in Nebraska is consistent with previously reported findings that small business owners thought that the handling of government regulation and red tape was a difficult and unexpected challenge for starting a business (see Table 4.10) and was one of the greatest non-financial obstacles to entrepreneurship (see Table 4.11).

Table 6.1: Government Regulation of Business[a]

Response	General Public (n=4,935)	Business Owners (n=1,122)
	%	%
Too much government regulation	59	70
Too little government regulation	8	4
About the right amount of government regulation	29	25
Don't know/Refused	6	1

Note: [a]"Thinking about government regulation of business, do you think there is:" [3][1]

A quarter (25%) of small business owners thought there was about the right amount of regulation. This ambivalent opinion about regulation among this minority of small business owners in Nebraska may reflect a desire for some rules and enforcement to bring order to business practices in the marketplace, or the fact that small business owners have the need for government protection in their roles as consumers of products purchased from other businesses.

The general public in Nebraska was surveyed on their opinions about government regulation using the same question. What is surprising is that their opinions are quite similar to those of small business owners in Nebraska. The majority (59%) of the general public also thought that there was too much regulation of business and very few (8%) thought there was too little regulation. Almost three in ten (29%) thought there was about the right amount of regulation. The results from the general public and business owners reveal strong opposition to the regulatory role of government.

One explanation can be offered for the similar responses of the general public and small business owners to the issue of regulation. The general public probably opposes government regulation in principle, especially when it is not apparent that the regulation affects them or has benefits for them. The general public, however, is likely to be more supportive of government regulation when its interests as consumers or buyers conflict with those of businesses as producers or sellers. Business owners are more opposed to government regulation probably because they feel the burden of it in operating their businesses and see few benefits.

Further probing on the issue of government regulation asked whether government regulations make it too difficult and expensive for people to start a business (Table 6.2). The general perception of both the general public and small business owners in Nebraska is that government regulations may be a hindrance to new business formation. As might be expected, small business owners show more agreement (67% either strongly agree or agree) than does the general public (56%), but nevertheless majorities in both groups see government regulation as a roadblock to the creation of new business ventures. Less than two in ten show any disagreement with the proposition.

Table 6.2:   Government Regulations Make It Too Difficult to Start a Business[a]

Response	General Public (n=2,475)	Business Owners (n=567)
	%	%
5 Strongly agree	34	44
4	22	23
3	22	13
2	10	12
1 Strongly disagree	7	7
Don't know/Refused	4	1

Note: [a]"Using a five-point scale, where 5 is strongly agree, and 1 is strongly disagree, please indicate if you agree or disagree with the following statement: Government regulations make it too difficult and expensive for many people to start a business." [2]

The issue of business taxes drew opposition from small business owners in Nebraska (Table 6.3). Almost two-thirds (64%) of small business owners thought that most businesses were overtaxed and few (6%) thought businesses were undertaxed. About three in ten (29%) thought businesses were taxed about the right amount. The largely negative view of taxes among small business owners in Nebraska was to be expected given the effect that such taxes have on increasing business costs and reducing profits.

Table 6.3: Business Taxes[a]

Response	General Public (n=4,935)	Business Owners (n=1,122)
	%	%
Overtaxed	42	64
Undertaxed	17	6
Taxed about the right amount	35	29
Don't know/Refused	8	3

Note: [a]"Thinking about taxes, do you think that most businesses are:" [3]

A smaller percentage of the general public than business owners (42% versus 64%) stated most businesses were overtaxed, while a larger percentage of the general public than business owners (17% versus 6%) stated that businesses were undertaxed. A plurality of the general public, however, thinks businesses are overtaxed. This opinion may reflect the generally negative views that most people have of taxes, regardless of whether they are personal or business taxes. It also suggests that there is some sympathy for business on the tax issue. The general public may show greater understanding of the adverse effects of taxation on business than might be expected given that much of the general public falls into the consumer, rather than the producer, side of most product issues.

As was the case with government regulation, further probing on the taxation issue was conducted to find out if people thought that taxes make it too difficult for people to start a business (Table 6.4). The general perception of both the general public and small business owners in Nebraska is that taxes make it difficult to start a new business, but the agreement among both

Table 6.4: Government Taxes Make It Too Difficult to Start a Business[a]

Response	General Public (n=2,475)	Business Owners (n=567)
	%	%
5 Strongly agree	32	35
4	19	21
3	24	22
2	12	15
1 Strongly disagree	8	8
Don't know/Refused	5	–

Note: [a]"Using a five-point scale, where 5 is strongly agree, and 1 is strongly disagree, please indicate if you agree or disagree with the following statement: Government taxes make it too difficult for many people to start a business." [2]

groups is less than the agreement expressed about the difficulties created for new business formation by government regulation (Table 6.2). As was the case with the same question about government regulation, small business owners showed more agreement (56% either strongly agree or agree) than did the general public (51%). Majorities in both groups also see taxation as another roadblock to the creation of new enterprises. Only about two in ten in each group expressed any disagreement with the proposition.

There may be general opposition among both the general public and small business owners in Nebraska on the issues of government regulation and taxation, but both groups think that government does have a role to play in helping to expand entrepreneurship. Only about three in ten (29%) of the general public and small business owners in Nebraska stated that government should provide no special help for people to start new businesses (Table 6.5), which implies that about seven in ten from each group would support such help or at least be open to having government provide it.

This finding also is supported by the results from a related question. As one option, most of the general public and small business owners gave their approval to the position that government should use its taxing authority to encourage entrepreneurship. About eight in ten (76–81%) of either group said yes to the policy of providing more tax incentives to people to start new businesses. The use of tax incentives may be more appealing because the expenditure is based on meeting a performance target and is not simply an allocation of tax dollars for a program with uncertain or unknown outcomes.

Table 6.5: What Government Should Do for Business[a]

Actions	Yes	No	DK
	%	%	%
A. Provide more tax incentives for people to start new businesses			
General Public (n=4935)	75	23	3
Business Owners (n=1122)	81	18	2
B. Provide more tax dollars for entrepreneurial education			
General Public	63	35	2
Business Owners	56	44	1
C. Provide more tax dollars to finance new business startups			
General Public	61	36	3
Business Owners	51	48	2
D. Provide no special help for people to start new businesses			
General Public	29	69	2
Business Owners	29	70	2

Note: [a]"Should government:" [3]

On other policy choices that involve providing tax dollars rather than tax incentives, there was less support among both groups and more of a split in the thinking of the general public and small business owners in Nebraska. Over half of each group recommended providing tax dollars for entrepreneurial education, but the support was higher among the general public (63%) than small business owners (56%). And, over half of each group thought that the government should provide more tax dollars to finance new business startups, but again, the support was greater among the general public (61%) than it was among small business owners (51%).

A major obstacle to starting a new business is obtaining the financing for it. In this area, most small business owners in Nebraska would rather rely on the private sector than on government (Table 6.6). When asked "Who should do more to improve the access to financing for people wanting to start a business?" less than half (46%) of business owners selected government as the vehicle for achieving this outcome. The predominant response, chosen by nine in ten (91%), was that banks should do more to improve access to financing. This option was followed next in support by local investors or venture capitalists (82%) and business organizations such as the chambers of commerce (72%). Whether banks are the right institution for financing entrepreneurship can be debated because banks may not want to assume risk for which there is uncertain collateral. The general point from the item is that the financing of startups is best left to the private sector.

Table 6.6: Who Should Improve Access to Financing[a]

Response: *Business Owners* (n=555)	Yes	No	DK
	%	%	%
Banks	91	9	0
Local investors/venture capitalists	82	17	1
Business organizations such as Chambers of Commerce	72	27	1
The government	46	52	1

Note: [a]"Who should do more to improve the access to financing for people wanting to start a business?" [1]

The above responses indicate that there is generally skepticism towards the role of government, especially as it pertains to stimulating entrepreneurship. This skepticism is probably healthy because it means that there will be public debate over the appropriate role of government in this area before actions are taken. It also indicates that whatever government can do to reduce the tax or regulatory burden for entrepreneurs would be viewed as a positive contribution to encouraging more entrepreneurship in the state.

A POSITIVE VIEW OF BUSINESS

In contrast to negative attitudes toward the role of government in the economy, the general public in Nebraska holds a positive view of small business. More than eight in ten (84%) Nebraskans supplied a positive response to this open-ended question asking for a feature they liked (Table 6.7). The most liked feature, cited by a third (33%), was the customer and personal service offered by small business. Other features cited, by much smaller percentages, were economic opportunity and freedom (25%), support for economic growth (17%), and competition and competitiveness (8%), or they gave other responses (1%). Almost two in ten of the general public gave either a "don't know" (14%) or a "nothing" (3%) response.

Table 6.7: Like Most about American Small Business[a]

Response	General Public (n=4,935)	Business Owners (n=1,122)
	%	%
Customer/personal service	33	7
Economic opportunity/freedom	25	68
Supports economic growth	17	10
Competitiveness and/or competition	8	9
Other	1	0
Total Citing a Positive Feature	**84**	**94**
Nothing	3	1
Don't know/Refused	14	5

Note: [a]"What do you like most about American small business?" [3]

More than nine in ten (94%) business owners stated a feature of small business that they liked. The largest percentage (68%) thought the most appealing feature was the economic opportunity and freedom it gave owners. The probable reason the perspective of small business owners differs from the general public is that small business owners likely thought about small business in terms of what it does for them as entrepreneurs, and therefore gave economic freedom and opportunity more importance. The general public looked at small business from their roles as consumers, and thus gave more emphasis to the customer and personal service aspects of it.

Another open-ended question requested the general public in Nebraska to state what they thought business owners contributed to the community where they were located (Table 6.8). Only one response was allowed, so it reflects the primary contributions in the minds of the general public. Most of the general public were aware of the economic contributions that business owners make to their communities. They were less likely to cite the philanthropic contribution that small business makes to a community.

Table 6.8: Contribution of Business Owners to Community[a]

Response	General Public (n=2,460)	
	%	%
Economic Factors		81
Provide jobs	31	
Help economic growth	23	
Offer new/quality products	13	
Give personal/friendly service	7	
Pay taxes	3	
Offer convenience/accessibility	2	
Add competition/control prices	2	
Philanthropic Factors		8
Contribute to charities/Establish charities	5	
Do public service work	3	
Other		3
Don't know/Refused		7
Nothing		2

Note: [a]"What, if anything, do you think business owners or entrepreneurs contribute to the community where they are located?" [1]

More than eight in ten (81%) cited an economic factor such as providing jobs (31%), helping economic growth (23%), offering new or quality products (13%), giving personal service (7%), paying taxes (3%), or some other factor (4%). Less often cited, by only about one in ten (8%) of the general public were the philanthropic contributions to a community, such as giving to or establishing charities (5%) or doing public service (3%). More than one in ten (12%) gave other reasons (3%), did not know (7%), or said nothing (2%).

The contribution question was posed in a different way in another question on the survey. This question asked how important it was for successful business owners or entrepreneurs to contribute something to the community *beyond providing jobs or paying taxes* (Table 6.9). Although the results from the previous two questions show that the general public in Nebraska holds a positive view of small business, the results from this question indicate that they have high expectations for businesses in their communities and want them to make a philanthropic contribution as well as an economic one.

Table 6.9: Importance of Community Contribution[a]

Response	General Public (n=4,935)	Business Owners (n=567)
	%	%
5 Very important	51	48
4	29	30
3	14	17
2	4	3
1 Not at all important	2	2
Don't know/Refused	1	1

Note: [a]"Using a five-point scale, where '5' is very important, and '1' is not at all important, how important do you think it is for successful business owners or entrepreneurs to contribute something to the community beyond providing jobs or paying taxes?" [3P, 2B]

There was strong agreement among the general public that businesses should give something back to the community beyond providing jobs. Eight in ten (80%) of the general public thought it was either *important* (29%) or *very important* (51%) for businesses to give something back to the community. What is interesting about the general public response is that they gave much greater weight to the very important response (51%) than the important response (29%) indicating that the general public highly values social responsibility in business.

The views of small business owners on this question are quite similar to those of the general public. Almost eight in ten (78%) of business owners thought it was either very important (48%) or important (30%) for business owners to contribute to a community beyond providing jobs or paying taxes. Very few businesses owners gave the opposite rating of not at all important (2%) or not important (3%) and few business owners were uncertain (17%).

A final question in this section sought to assess the degree of agreement among the general public and small business owners about the likely motivations for making a contribution to the community by business owners or entrepreneurs. Two of the three possibilities were polar opposites. One reason for giving was simply altruistic: they want to help the community. The other reason was pecuniary: they wanted to promote their business. The results (Table 6.10) show a split opinion among both the general public and business owners about the altruistic reasons. The great majority of each group (78%) stated that the altruistic reason of wanting to help the community was a *major* reason for giving by business owners or entrepreneurs. Almost the same percentages from each group (74–75%), however, also stated that a major reason for giving was to promote their business.

Table 6.10: Motivations for Community Contribution[a]

Reasons[b]	Major	Minor	Not
	%	%	%
They want to help the community			
General Public (n=2,475)	78	18	3
Business Owners (n=567)	78	19	2
They want to promote their business			
General Public	75	20	2
Business Owners	74	23	2
It is tax deductible			
General Public	49	39	8
Business Owners	42	44	13

Notes:
[a]"For each of the possible reasons a business owner or entrepreneur might have for contributing to the community beyond providing jobs or paying taxes, do you think it would be a major reason, a minor reason, or not a reason at all?" [2]
[b]Don't know responses were omitted in the table.

The third reason also was pecuniary, but it was different in that it reflected the influence of government policy through tax benefits. Both the general public and business owners expressed a significantly mixed opinion about whether the tax deductibility of charitable contributions by business owners or entrepreneurs was the motivating factor in community giving. About half (49%) of the general public responded that this was a major reason for giving, but about half (47%) also replied that it was a minor reason or not a reason. Business owners were less likely to think it was a major reason (42%) and more likely to think it was either a minor reason or not a reason (57%). The majority of business owners gave less credence to this factor as a reason for community giving compared with the responses of the general public, perhaps because the tax benefits were relatively minor. Business promotion, or having a good reputation in a community, was clearly the more dominant pecuniary reason for giving by businesses, and this reason was recognized about equally by business owners and the general public.

ECONOMIC DEVELOPMENT ISSUES

Most communities in Nebraska are concerned about improving business and economic conditions as a way to provide economic growth, greater incomes, and more jobs in the local areas. Such activity is generally discussed under the term economic development. The development activity can come from initiative in the public sector, the private sector, or some combination.

A first question to be asked on the issue of economic development is whether people consider there is a generally positive or negative climate for business and entrepreneurship in their communities (Table 6.11). The results from asking the general public about this business climate in their communities show that the outlook of most Nebraskans is relatively positive. Almost half of the general public (46%) and half (50%) of small business owners said that the climate for business and entrepreneurship in their communities was either *very positive* or *positive*. By contrast, few members of the general public (16%) or business owners (20%) held negative opinions about the climate for business and entrepreneurship in the communities in which they lived. These generally positive attitudes are consistent with the other favorable views about business that were reported in the previous section and also consistent with positive attitudes toward entrepreneurship presented in Chapters 4 and 5.

Table 6.11: Positive or Negative Climate for Business[a]

Response	General Public (n=2,475)	Business Owners (n=567)
	%	%
5 Very positive	17	16
4	29	34
3	36	29
2	10	15
1 Very negative	6	5
Don't know/Refused	0	2

Note: [a]"Using a five-point scale, where 5 is very positive, and 1 is very negative, how would you rate the climate for business and entrepreneurship in your community?" [2]

The climate question is more of a measure of the openness of a community to business or entrepreneurship. It does not assess whether a community is being effective in improving or developing its resource base. To assess such views another question was asked that directly focuses on whether economic development efforts in general were effective in communities (Table 6.12). Both the general public and the business owners groups surveyed were representative samples of their respective populations in Nebraska so their responses would provide a reasonably accurate perspective about this economic development work across the state. The question asked of each group was a general one that did not specify whether the economic development efforts in a community were public, private, or some combination of the two.

Table 6.12: Effectiveness of Economic Development[a]

Response	General Public (n=4,935)	Business Owners (n=1,122)
	%	%
5 Very effective	13	11
4	29	23
3	35	32
2	13	20
1 Very ineffective	9	15
Don't know/Refused	3	2

Note: [a]"Using a five-point scale, where '5' is very effective, and '1' is very ineffective, how would you rate the economic development efforts in your community?" [3]

The responses showed relatively limited satisfaction with the economic development efforts in most communities. About a third (34%) of small business owners in Nebraska rated economic development efforts in their communities as being either *very effective* (11%) or *effective* (23%) Another third (35%) rated it as either very ineffective (15%) or ineffective (20%) Another third (32%) of small business owners were uncertain. These results are hardly a strong endorsement of what is going on in the name of economic development in various communities in Nebraska.

The views of the general public were slightly more favorable than those of small business owners, but not to a great degree. Among this group, more than four in ten (42%) rated the economic development efforts as either very effective or effective. By contrast, more than two in ten (22%) thought the efforts were very ineffective or ineffective, and a third (35%) was uncertain. So even among this group, the majority (57%) gave an uncertain or negative rating to the economic development efforts in their communities. The survey responses from both groups show deep concern about this activity for stimulating new business and economic growth in Nebraska communities.

There are other issues that can create potential problems for starting a business in Nebraska (Table 6.13). Both small business owners and the general public in Nebraska hold about the same perceptions of whether an issue is a major problem for starting a business. At the top of the list of major problems is the cost of health care, which was cited by about eight in ten (79–81%) of both groups. The next problem drawing the most response was the burden of state and local taxes, which drew responses from about six in ten (62–63%) of both groups. The taxation problem also was a major concern that was discussed in the responses to several questions in the first section of the chapter (see Tables 6.3 and 6.4).

Table 6.13: Major Problems for Starting a Business[a]

Issues	Yes	No	DK
	%	%	%
A. Cost of health care			
General Public (n=2,475)	79	18	1
Business Owners (n=567)	81	19	0
B. State and local taxes			
General Public	62	33	5
Business Owners	63	38	–
C. Poor economic conditions			
General Public	46	50	4
Business Owners	49	51	0
D. Finding workers			
General Public	37	60	3
Business Owners	49	51	–
E. A negative climate for business			
General Public	38	58	4
Business Owners	37	63	0

Note: [a]"Which of the following do you think is a major problem or challenge in Nebraska that prevents people from starting a business? Please respond by saying 'yes' or 'no'." [2]

The other problems drew less than a majority of each group, which suggests that they are of less importance than health care and taxes. Less than five in ten (46–49%) stated that poor economic conditions in Nebraska were a major problem. Similarly, less than four in ten (37–38%) felt there was a negative climate for business that restricted entrepreneurship, which is consistent with the generally favorable views on business climate reported in a previous question (Table 6.11). The only problem on which there was a slight difference was the one of finding workers. Predictably, more business owners stated it was a problem than did the general public probably because the business owners had more direct experience with labor shortages. About half (49%) of business owners considered this employment issue to be a major problem compared with just over a third (37%) of the general public.

Both groups were asked whether they thought it was positive or negative for a new business to come into a community and compete with existing businesses (Table 6.14). Although a plurality of both groups stated that the development was a positive one, the responses were not as positive as might be expected. In fact, small business owners appeared more concerned with this development than did the general public. Only about a third (36%) of small business owners viewed this development as a positive one compared with four in ten (44%) of the general public.

Table 6.14: Perception of New Competing Business[a]

Response	General Public (n=4,935)	Business Owners (n=1,122)
	%	%
5 Very positive	19	16
4	25	20
3	34	36
2	13	18
1 Very negative	8	11
Don't know/Refused	3	1

Note: [a]"A business wants to come into your community, but it would compete with several existing businesses. Using a five-point scale, where 5 is very positive, and 1 is very negative, how positive or negative is this development?" [3]

Perhaps the reason for this weak positive response to this natural feature of a market economy was that each group is worried about the adverse effects of the new competitor to existing businesses. Small business owners were more concerned than the public because they had more to lose in this case than did members of the general public, who may benefit if the new competing business brings lower prices and a wider variety of product or service choices. Nevertheless, increased competition is part of the dynamic of a market economy and a vital part of economic landscapes for future economic growth in communities. More economic competition should not be feared and thus lead to an attempt to protect or restrict local markets and keep out competitors. The focus of economic development should be proactive to attract new businesses rather than protectionist and reactive.

The discussion so far has focused on ways to encourage individuals to become entrepreneurs and ways to attract or stimulate the formation of new businesses in communities. But entrepreneurship flows two ways. At any point in time, people both enter into entrepreneurship by starting businesses, and they exit by ending a business or transferring it to others to continue. These inflows and outflows have a significant effect on economic development in communities and raise concerns about business succession.

The outflow is clearly a challenge for Nebraska (Table 6.15). Small business owners in Nebraska were asked a simple question: "In how many years do you plan to exit your business?" The results are surprising and indicate that there are serious problems facing the Nebraska economy. Almost one in three (29%) small business owners in Nebraska said they planned to exit the businesses during the next five years. About another quarter (23%) said they expect to exit their businesses in six to ten years. Taken together the two responses indicate that over half (52%) of small business owners will be gone over the next ten years. This percentage also does not take into account the one in ten (10%) who did not know or who did not give a response. Many in this group may want to exit the business in the next ten years. Only slightly more than a third (38%) indicated they would be in business for a period of time longer than ten years.

Table 6.15: Years to Exit Business[a]

Response	Business Owners (n=1,122)
0–5	29%
6–10	23
11–15	10
More than 15 years	28
Don't know/Refused	10

Note: [a]"In how many years do you plan to exit your business?" [3]

What needs to be understood is that entrepreneurship is a changing process that is neither stable nor permanent. Businesses come and go in communities because entrepreneurs come and go. The only way a community can revitalize its economy and continue to grow is to make sure that inflow to entrepreneurship is greater than the outflow from it. The answer to that question is a yet unresolved one for Nebraska. Should the inflow be less than the outflow, then there could be severe adverse consequences for the Nebraska economy and local communities that depend on entrepreneurial initiatives for future economic growth, jobs creation, and incomes. Economic development efforts in local communities will need to address this issue of how to attract new business owners to replace existing business owners.

A related issue is to whom a business would be transferred should an entrepreneur want to exit a business (Table 6.16). If existing businesses are taken over by other people, then the entrepreneurial leakage is stemmed to a certain degree. The results from the transfer question suggest that type of outcome will occur in most cases. Over a third (36%) of small business owners plan to transfer the business operation to a family member. Business succession typically occurs within a family, but it is a process that can be difficult and challenging without sufficient planning. Almost two in ten (19%) would sell it to a third party and one in ten (10%) would sell it to an employee or employees. These other two options also merit further study to see if there are other ways to attract new entrepreneurs to communities to take over businesses or to help more employees prepare for the possibility of becoming business owners.

Table 6.16: Who to Transfer Business to[a]

Response	Business Owners (n=1,122)
Family	36%
Employee(s)	10
Third party	19
Liquidate	25
Don't know/Refused/Other	11

Note: [a]"Who do you plan on transferring your business to?" [3]

What is especially troubling is that a quarter (25%) said they would liquidate the business. These results suggest that these owners either have no viable opportunities to continue their businesses or that the businesses have insufficient value in their current forms and would bring more value if liquidated. The effects of such liquidations can harm the Nebraska communities and dampen the climate for future entrepreneurship. Business transition and succession are economic development issues that can adversely affect entrepreneurship in Nebraska. They deserve more study to find creative ways to increase the pool of potential entrepreneurs and attract new business owners to local communities in Nebraska.

COMPARISONS: COMMUNITY COLLEGE REGIONS, BUSINESS SIZE, AND NATIONAL

Appendix 6A reports the results to all the survey questions in this chapter for the general public based on location in a community college district (see Figure 2.4 for the district map). Some interesting differences among the regions on views of government are worth highlighting. On the issue of government regulation of business (Table 6.1a), the general public in the four districts outside the Omaha or Lincoln metro areas (Central, Northeast, Mid-Plains, and Western) are more likely to think there is too much government regulation (63–65%) than do the other two districts (Southeast: 57%; Metropolitan: 54%). While the majority throughout the state are opposed to government regulation, there is greater opposition in the more rural regions. This subtle difference also is shown in responses to the question of whether government regulations make it too difficult to start a business (Table 6.2a). Only about five in ten of the general public in the Metropolitan (52%) and Southeast (55%) districts strongly agree or agree with this statement compared with about six in ten (59% to 64%) in the other districts.

A similar split in opinion occurs with views about taxes on businesses ((Table 6.3a). Smaller percentages of the general public (39%) think most businesses are overtaxed in the Metropolitan and Southeast regions than do residents in the Central (44%), Northeast (49%), Mid-Plains (49%), and Western (51%) regions. There also is a comparable split of opinion on the related question of whether taxes make it too difficult to start a business (Table 6.4a), at least when considering the strongly agree responses (28–30% versus 35–40%), although it is less pronounced when combining agree and strongly agree responses (48–51% versus 52–59%).

As for what government should do to help to promote entrepreneurship (Table 6.5a), the results show general agreement across all districts. More than seven in ten (73–78%) of Nebraskans, regardless of the district in which they reside, think that government should provide more tax incentives for people to start new businesses. About six in ten in each district support having the government provide more tax dollars for entrepreneurship education (60–69%) or provide more tax dollars to finance new business startups (59–64%). Some type of action by government to promote entrepreneurship is favored to some degree in each district because only about three in ten (28–34%) in each district thought government should provide no special help for people to start new businesses.

Views of business are quite similar across the districts (Table 6.7a). More than eight in ten (82–87%) of the general public in each district could cite a positive feature that they liked about small business such as personal service, economic opportunity and freedom, or support for economic growth. Also, most respondents in each district (77–83%) thought that it was either very important or important for successful business owners to contribute something to the community beyond providing jobs or paying taxes (Table 6.9a). Most Nebraskans in each region also ascribed both altruistic motives (they want to help the community: 73–83%) and pecuniary reasons (they want to promote their businesses: 73–79%) for these contributions.

Some contrasts are revealed in several other questions. More residents in the Metropolitan district either strongly agreed or agreed (52%) that there was a positive climate for business than did residents in other districts (35–44%) (Table 6.11a). More residents in the Metropolitan district (49%) and the Central district (44%) than the residents in other four districts (32–38%) stated that economic development efforts were either very effective or effective (Table 6.12a). The strong economic growth in the Omaha area may account for these positive views of the business climate and economic development in the Metropolitan district.

Opinions about the major problems for starting a business show substantial variation across districts (Table 6.13a). The greatest contrasts are between Nebraskans in the Metropolitan district and the Western district on whether there is a major problem for entrepreneurship from poor economic conditions (35% versus 65%), finding workers (31% versus 51%), or a negative climate for business (33% versus 44%). The differences are less extreme, but still pronounced regarding the cost of health care (77% versus 81%) or state and local taxes (62% versus 71%). Among all the districts, the major problems for starting a business that received the most citations were the cost of health care (77–81%) and state and local taxes (60–71%).

Appendix 6B displays the findings when the business owner responses are separated by the size of the firm. On the issue of government regulation of business the perceptions of most small business owners, regardless of firm size, are similar in that over two-thirds (67–73%) in each group stated that there is too much regulation (Table 6.1b). Likewise, about two-thirds (64–74%) in each group also stated that government regulation makes it too difficult and expensive for many people to start a business (Table 6.2b).

The opinions about taxes on businesses are about the same as views of government regulation of businesses. More than six in ten (62–70%) of business owners by firm size stated that businesses are overtaxed (Table 6.3b). About five in ten (51–58%) business owners by firm size said that taxes make it too difficult to start a business (Table 6.4b).

The differences in the views of business owners by firm size are more striking in the responses to questions about what government should do to promote entrepreneurship (Table 6.5b). Owners of firms with the fewest number of employees (1–10) compared with owners of firms with the most employees (50–100) are more likely to want tax incentives for people to start new businesses (82% versus 73%), more tax dollars for entrepreneurship education (57% versus 50%), and more tax dollars to finance new businesses (51% versus 44%).

The owners of the smallest firms compared with the owners of the largest firms also are more likely to state that improvement of financing for starting new businesses should come from organizations such as chambers of commerce (73% versus 64%) or from the government (47% versus 24%) (Table 6.6b). The owners of the largest firms were more likely to cite the need for improved access to financing from local investors or venture capitalists compared with owners of smaller firms (92% versus 81–86%).

When asked to state what they liked most about American small business, about nine in ten (from 93% to 96%) in each group of business owners cited a positive feature, and for the great majority of business owners (61–69%) the featured cited most often was economic opportunity and freedom (Table 6.7b). There was little disagreement about the importance of successful businesses to make contributions to the community beyond providing jobs or paying taxes because about three-fourths or more (74–82%) considered it to be *important* or *very important* (Table 6.9b). There were only minor differences in views about the motivations for this community giving as being altruistic (79–86%) or for promotion (69–74%) (Table 6.10b).

About half (46–53%) of business owners by firm size stated that there is a very positive or positive climate for business (Table 6.11b). A substantially smaller percentage in each group (33–43%) also thought that economic development efforts in local communities were very effective or effective, with owners of the smallest firms being the least positive (33%) and owners of the largest firms being the most positive (43%).

A similar contrast between the views of owners of the smallest- and largest-sized business firms was found in responses to a question with a list of major problems for starting a business (Table 6.13b). The owners of the smallest firms were more likely than owners of the largest firms to state there were major problems or challenges for entrepreneurship from the cost of health care (84% versus 77%), poor economic conditions (50% versus 29%), or a negative climate for business (38% versus 26%). Owners of the largest businesses, however, were more likely to cite state and local taxes as being a major problem than were owners of the smallest firms (74% versus 62%), perhaps because they had more experience with the burden of taxation on businesses.

There is remarkable similarity in responses among business owners by firm size on the issue of how many years it will be before they exit the business (Table 6.15b). About half in each group (51–54%) state it will be in ten years or less. About a third (31–36%) of the business owners in each group plan to transfer the business to a family member when they leave the business, but there is substantial variation in responses to the other options (Table 6.16b). Most noteworthy is that about a quarter (26%) of owners of the smallest firms plan to liquidate compared with only about one in ten (8–12%) in the other business groups. The results suggest that keeping the smallest businesses in communities may be a challenging problem for the issue of business succession.

A few comparisons can be made with national findings as shown in Appendix 6C. On the issue of government regulation of business, both the general public and small business owners in Nebraska are more critical than their counterparts nationwide and state there is too much regulation (59% versus 50% for the general public and 70% versus 56% for small business owners) (Table 6.1c).   On the issue of taxation of businesses, there is similarity in the opinions held by the general public that businesses are overtaxed (42% versus 46%), but this opinion is held by less than half of each group.   As might be expected, business owners are more likely than the general public to think businesses are overtaxed, but this position is more strongly held at the national level than the state level (71% versus 64%).

Ratings of the importance of business contributions to a community (Table 6.9c) are essentially equivalent for each group at the state and national levels. There are, however, a few differences on the motivations question that are striking for the general public. Nebraska adults appear to be less cynical than adults nationwide about the motivating reasons for why businesses contribute to communities (Table 6.10c). Fewer Nebraska adults than adults nationwide thought that businesses made contributions to communities just to promote their businesses (75% versus 85%) or just as a tax deduction (49% versus 60%). Conversely, more Nebraska adults than adults nationwide thought that businesses made contributions because they wanted to help the community (78% versus 58%). The views of business owners at the state and national levels on the motivating reasons for contributions are about the same for each of the three categories.

CONCLUSION

This chapter covered a broad range of issues that can affect the climate for entrepreneurship and business in Nebraska. Among the major findings from the survey investigation are the following:

- The role of government in fostering entrepreneurship is viewed with skepticism by the general public and small business owners in Nebraska. There is general consensus that any help given to promote entrepreneurship in the state should be done with tax incentives instead of tax dollar expenditures for programs.
- Nebraskans hold a positive view of small business. They like the customer and personal service and the economic contributions it makes to the state; small business owners like the economic opportunity and freedom it provides.
- Successful business owners in Nebraska have a responsibility to give back to their communities in the opinion of both the general public and small business owners. The reasons for such giving may be altruistic or promotional, but whatever the motivation, the contribution is important.

- There is an overall positive view of the climate for entrepreneurship and business in local communities, but economic development efforts in communities are viewed as being generally ineffective by both the general public and small business owners in Nebraska.
- Nebraska faces problems with business succession and transitions in business ownership because about half of the current owners plan to exit their businesses in the next ten years and some businesses may liquidate in the process.

The broad understanding to be gained is that opinions and perceptions about government, small business, and economic development are likely to influence attitudes toward entrepreneurship and the willingness to start new businesses. Such views and perspectives are worthy of study because they are likely to affect the pool of potential entrepreneurs in Nebraska and also the entrepreneurial environment in the state.

NOTES

1. At the end of each question for each table is a code in square brackets: The [1] refers to items given only in the 2005 survey. The code [2] refers to items given only in the 2006 survey. The code [3] refers to a survey given both years. If a survey was given to one group but not another in a particular year, the code includes a symbol for either the general public (P) or small business owners (B) to indicate that group distinction for a survey item.

APPENDIX 6A: General Public by Community College

Table 6.1a: Government Regulation of Business[a] *(n=4,935)*

	Community College District					
	Metro-politan	South-east	Central	North-east	Mid-Plains	Western
Response	(n=819)	(801)	(807)	(827)	(858)	(823)
	%	%	%	%	%	%
Too much government regulation	54	57	63	63	64	65
Too little government regulation	9	9	5	6	6	6
About the right amount of government regulation	31	29	26	27	25	24
Don't know/Refused	6	6	6	5	5	5

Note: [a]"Thinking about government regulation of business, do you think there is:" [3]

Table 6.2a: Government Regulations Make It Too Difficult to Start a Business[a] *(n=2,475)*

	Community College District					
	Metro-politan	South-east	Central	North-east	Mid-Plains	Western
Response	(n=400)	(402)	(400)	(415)	(454)	(404)
	%	%	%	%	%	%
5 Strongly agree	31	32	38	38	41	44
4	21	23	21	23	21	23
3	25	21	22	19	19	18
2	12	10	11	8	6	10
1 Strongly disagree	7	10	6	7	9	2
Don't know/Refused	4	4	3	5	4	3

Note: [a]"Using a five-point scale, where 5 is strongly agree, and 1 is strongly disagree, please indicate if you agree or disagree with the following statement: Government regulations make it too difficult and expensive for many people to start a business." [2]

Table 6.3a: Business Taxes[a] (n=4,935)

Response	Community College District					
	Metro-politan (n=819)	South-east (801)	Central (807)	North-east (827)	Mid-Plains (858)	Western (823)
	%	%	%	%	%	%
Overtaxed	39	39	44	49	49	51
Undertaxed	20	19	12	9	9	10
Taxed about the right amount	34	35	37	35	36	33
Don't know/Refused	8	8	6	8	6	7

Note: [a]"Thinking about taxes, do you think that most businesses are:" [3]

Table 6.4a: Government Taxes Make It Too Difficult to Start a Business[a] (n=2,475)

Response	Community College District					
	Metro-politan (n=400)	South-east (402)	Central (400)	North-east (415)	Mid-Plains (454)	Western (404)
	%	%	%	%	%	%
5 Strongly agree	30	28	35	40	36	40
4	21	20	17	19	18	19
3	24	23	26	21	24	25
2	13	13	12	7	9	9
1 Strongly disagree	8	11	6	8	10	4
Don't know/Refused	5	5	5	5	4	3

Note: [a]"Using a five-point scale, where 5 is strongly agree, and 1 is strongly disagree, please indicate if you agree or disagree with the following statement: Government taxes make it too difficult for many people to start a business." [2]

Table 6.5a: What Government Should Do for Business[a] *(n=4,935)*

Actions	Yes	No	DK
	%	%	%
Provide more tax incentives for people to start new businesses			
Metropolitan CC (n=819)	75	23	2
Southeast CC (n=801)	73	25	2
Central CC (n=807)	78	20	3
Northeast CC (n=827)	75	22	3
Mid-Plains CC (n=858)	77	22	2
Western CC (n=823)	75	23	2
Provide more tax dollars for entrepreneurial education			
Metropolitan CC	60	37	3
Southeast CC	63	35	2
Central CC	66	32	2
Northeast CC	69	28	4
Mid-Plains CC	62	35	3
Western CC	63	34	3
Provide more tax dollars to finance new business startups			
Metropolitan CC	60	38	3
Southeast CC	61	37	2
Central CC	62	35	3
Northeast CC	64	33	3
Mid-Plains CC	59	37	3
Western CC	60	37	4
Provide no special help for people to start new businesses			
Metropolitan CC	28	70	2
Southeast CC	30	68	2
Central CC	28	70	2
Northeast CC	34	63	3
Mid-Plains CC	30	66	3
Western CC	32	66	3

Note: [a]"Should government:" [3]

Table 6.7a: *Like Most about American Small Business*[a] (n=4,935)

	Community College District					
Response	Metro-politan (n=819)	South-east (801)	Central (807)	North-east (827)	Mid-Plains (858)	Western (823)
	%	%	%	%	%	%
Customer/personal service	28	35	37	31	35	35
Economic opportunity/ freedom	26	28	23	24	22	26
Supports economic growth	18	17	17	18	17	16
Competitiveness and/or competition	9	6	7	7	9	8
Other	1	1	1	2	1	1
Total Citing a Positive Feature	**82**	**87**	**85**	**82**	**84**	**86**
Nothing	3	2	2	3	3	2
Don't know/Refused	15	12	12	16	13	12

Note: [a]"What do you like most about American small business?" [3]

Table 6.9a: *Importance of Community Contribution*[a] (n=4,935)

	Community College District					
Response	Metro-politan (n=819)	South-east (801)	Central (807)	North-east (827)	Mid-Plains (858)	Western (823)
	%	%	%	%	%	%
5 Very important	48	51	54	54	53	49
4	29	30	29	25	27	33
3	16	14	12	13	13	13
2	3	3	3	3	4	2
1 Not at all important	1	2	1	2	2	2
Don't know/Refused	2	1	1	3	2	1

Note: [a]"Using a five-point scale, where "5" is very important, and "1" is not at all important, how important do you think it is for successful business owners or entrepreneurs to contribute something to the community beyond providing jobs or paying taxes?" [3]

Table 6.10a: Motivations for Community Contribution[a] *(n=2,475)*

Reasons[b]	Major	Minor	Not
	%	%	%
They want to help the community			
Metropolitan CC (n=400)	73	22	3
Southeast CC (n=402)	78	18	3
Central CC (n=400)	83	13	2
Northeast CC (n=415)	81	15	3
Mid-Plains CC (n=454)	80	17	1
Western CC (n=404)	81	17	2
They want to promote their business			
Metropolitan CC	76	19	4
Southeast CC	74	21	2
Central CC	74	19	6
Northeast CC	73	22	4
Mid-Plains CC	79	14	4
Western CC	78	17	4
It is tax deductible			
Metropolitan CC	49	39	10
Southeast CC	51	38	7
Central CC	45	43	9
Northeast CC	49	38	8
Mid-Plains CC	49	38	8
Western CC	51	38	8

Notes:
[a]"For each of the possible reasons a business owner or entrepreneur might have for contributing to the community beyond providing jobs or paying taxes, do you think it would be a major reason, a minor reason, or not a reason at all?" [2]
[b]Don't know responses were omitted in the table.

Table 6.11a: Positive or Negative Climate for Business[a] *(n=2,475)*

	Community College District					
	Metro-politan	South-east	Central	North-east	Mid-Plains	Western
Response	(n=400)	(402)	(400)	(415)	(454)	(404)
	%	%	%	%	%	%
5 Very positive	19	15	15	17	16	13
4	33	29	25	24	28	22
3	37	34	38	37	33	31
2	3	12	15	13	12	23
1 Very negative	5	7	5	7	7	9
Don't know/Refused	4	4	3	3	4	3

Note: [a]"Using a five-point scale, where 5 is very positive, and 1 is very negative, how would you rate the climate for business and entrepreneurship in your community?" [2]

Table 6.12a: Effectiveness of Economic Development[a] (n=4,935)

Response	Community College District					
	Metro-politan (n=819)	South-east (801)	Central (807)	North-east (827)	Mid-Plains (858)	Western (823)
	%	%	%	%	%	%
5 Very effective	14	10	17	13	11	10
4	35	24	27	25	27	22
3	35	39	32	33	33	32
2	8	15	14	15	15	21
1 Very ineffective	6	10	8	11	12	14
Don't know/Refused	3	4	2	3	2	1

Note: [a]"Using a five-point scale, where '5' is very effective, and '1' is very ineffective, how would you rate the economic development efforts in your community?" [3]

Table 6.13a: Major Problems for Starting a Business[a] *(n=2,475)*

Response	Yes	No	DK
	%	%	%
Cost of health care			
Metropolitan CC (n=400)	77	20	4
Southeast CC (n=402)	76	21	3
Central CC (n=400)	81	16	3
Northeast CC (n=415)	83	12	5
Mid-Plains CC (n=454)	80	18	3
Western CC (n=404)	81	17	2
State and local taxes			
Metropolitan CC	62	34	5
Southeast CC	60	36	5
Central CC	65	31	4
Northeast CC	63	31	7
Mid-Plains CC	62	34	5
Western CC	71	25	4
Poor economic conditions			
Metropolitan CC	35	61	4
Southeast CC	47	51	3
Central CC	50	48	2
Northeast CC	63	32	6
Mid-Plains CC	60	37	3
Western CC	65	32	4
Finding workers			
Metropolitan CC	31	65	4
Southeast CC	35	63	2
Central CC	42	56	3
Northeast CC	45	50	5
Mid-Plains CC	46	51	3
Western CC	51	47	2
A negative climate for business			
Metropolitan CC	33	64	4
Southeast CC	38	59	4
Central CC	39	57	4
Northeast CC	47	47	6
Mid-Plains CC	46	50	4
Western CC	44	52	4

Note: [a]"Which of the following do you think is a major problem or challenge in Nebraska that prevents people from starting a business? Please respond by saying 'yes' or 'no'." [2]

Table 6.14a: Perception of New Competing Business[a] (n=4,935)

Response	Community College District					
	Metro-politan (n=819)	South-east (801)	Central (807)	North-east (827)	Mid-Plains (858)	Western (823)
	%	%	%	%	%	%
5 Very positive	18	19	20	16	19	20
4	28	22	23	20	22	23
3	35	34	31	37	31	31
2	11	13	14	13	14	14
1 Very negative	5	8	10	10	11	10
Don't know/Refused	3	3	2	3	3.	3

Note: [a]"A business wants to come into your community, but it would compete with several existing businesses. Using a five-point scale, where 5 is very positive, and 1 is very negative, how positive or negative is this development?" [3]

APPENDIX 6B: Business Owners by Number of Employees

Table 6.1b: Government Regulation of Business[a] (n=1,122)

	Number of Employees			
	1–10	**11–19**	**20–49**	**50–100**
Response	(n=322)	(314)	(296)	(190)
	%	%	%	%
Too much government regulation	70	73	76	67
Too little government regulation	4	5	3	4
About the right amount of government regulation	25	22	20	27
Don't know/Refused	1	0	0	1

Note: [a]"Thinking about government regulation of business, do you think there is:" [3]

Table 6.2b: Government Regulations Make It Too Difficult to Start a Business[a] (n=567)

	Number of Employees			
	1–10	**11–19**	**20–49**	**50–100**
Response	(n=172)	(162)	(146)	(87)
	%	%	%	%
5 Strongly agree	47	41	37	44
4	22	33	30	20
3	13	16	19	24
2	11	6	8	12
1 Strongly disagree	6	4	8	1
Don't know/Refused	1	0	0	0

Note: [a]"Using a five-point scale, where 5 is strongly agree, and 1 is strongly disagree, please indicate if you agree or disagree with the following statement: Government regulations make it too difficult and expensive for many people to start a business." [2]

Table 6.3b: Business Taxes[a] (n=1,122)

Response	Number of Employees			
	1–10	11–19	20–49	50–100
	(n=322)	(314)	(296)	(190)
	%	%	%	%
Overtaxed	63	70	65	62
Undertaxed	6	3	4	4
Taxed about the right amount	29	26	29	32
Don't know/Refused	1	0	1	1

Note: [a]"Thinking about taxes, do you think that most businesses are:" [3]

Table 6.4b: Government Taxes Make It Too Difficult to Start a Business[a] (n=567)

Response	Number of Employees			
	1–10	11–19	20–49	50–100
	(n=172)	(162)	(146)	(87)
	%	%	%	%
5 Strongly agree	36	36	30	30
4	20	22	21	22
3	23	24	27	26
2	14	13	13	17
1 Strongly disagree	7	6	9	5

Note: [a]"Using a five-point scale, where 5 is strongly agree, and 1 is strongly disagree, please indicate if you agree or disagree with the following statement: Government taxes make it too difficult for many people to start a business." [2]

Table 6.5b: What Government Should Do for Business[a] (n=1,122)

Actions	Yes	No	DK
	%	%	%
Provide more tax incentives for people to start new businesses			
1–10 employees (n=322)	82	17	2
11–19 employees (n=314)	76	23	1
20–49 employees (n=296)	72	27	1
50–100 employees (n=190)	73	27	0
Provide more tax dollars for entrepreneurial education			
1–10 employees	57	43	1
11–19 employees	55	43	2
20–49 employees	48	51	1
50–100 employees	50	51	0
Provide more tax dollars to finance new business startups			
1–10 employees	51	47	2
11–19 employees	49	50	1
20–49 employees	44	55	0
50–100 employees	44	55	1
Provide no special help for people to start new businesses			
1–10 employees	27	71	2
11–19 employees	34	65	1
20–49 employees	32	67	1
50–100 employees	34	64	2

Note: [a]"Should government:" [3]

Table 6.6b: Who Should Improve Access to Financing[a] (n=555)

Response	Yes	No	DK
	%	%	%
A. Banks			
1–10 employees (n=150)	91	9	0
11–19 employees (n=152)	94	6	0
20–49 employees (n=179)	90	9	1
50–100 employees (n=74)	92	8	0
B. Local investors/venture capitalists			
1–10 employees	81	17	1
11–19 employees	86	13	1
20–49 employees	83	16	1
50–100 employees	92	8	0
C. Business organizations such as Chambers of Commerce			
1–10 employees	73	26	1
11–19 employees	62	37	1
20–49 employees	64	35	1
50–100 employees	64	37	0
D. The government			
1–10 employees	47	51	1
11–19 employees	38	61	2
20–49 employees	41	59	0
50–100 employees	24	76	0

Note: [a]"Who should do more to improve the access to financing for people wanting to start a business?" [1]

Table 6.7b: Like Most about American Small Business[a] (n=1,122)

	Number of Employees			
	1–10	**11–19**	**20–49**	**50–100**
Response	(n=322)	(314)	(296)	(190)
	%	%	%	%
Customer/personal service	7	6	4	5
Economic opportunity/freedom	69	62	63	61
Supports economic growth	9	13	14	16
Competitiveness/competition	8	12	14	12
Other	0	1	1	2
Total Citing a Positive Feature	93	94	96	96
Nothing	1	2	1	2
Don't know/Refused	5	4	3	3

Note: [a]"What do you like most about American small business?" [3]

Table 6.9b: Importance of Community Contribution[a] (n=567)

	Number of Employees			
	1–10	11–19	20–49	50–100
Response	(n=172)	(162)	(146)	(87)
	%	%	%	%
5 Very important	46	43	40	47
4	32	32	34	35
3	15	17	19	15
2	5	6	5	2
1 Not at all important	2	3	1	0
Don't know/Refused	1	0	0	1

Note: [a]"Using a five-point scale, where "5" is very important, and "1" is not at all important, how important do you think it is for successful business owners or entrepreneurs to contribute something to the community beyond providing jobs or paying taxes?" [2]

Table 6.10b: Motivations for Community Contribution[a] (n=567)

Reasons[b]	Major	Minor	Not
	%	%	%
They want to help the community			
1–10 employees (n=172)	79	18	2
11–19 employees (n=162)	74	21	4
20–49 employees (n=146)	84	15	1
50–100 employees (n=87)	86	13	1
They want to promote their business			
1–10 employees	74	23	2
11–19 employees	75	19	5
20–49 employees	65	27	7
50–100 employees	69	24	7
It is tax deductible			
1–10 employees	42	44	13
11–19 employees	38	54	8
20–49 employees	43	46	10
50–100 employees	30	60	10

Notes:
[a]"For each of the possible reasons a business owner or entrepreneur might have for contributing to the community beyond providing jobs or paying taxes, do you think it would be a major reason, a minor reason, or not a reason at all?" [2]
[b]Don't know responses were omitted in the table.

Table 6.11b: Positive or Negative Climate for Business[a] (n=567)

Response	Number of Employees			
	1–10	**11–19**	**20–49**	**50–100**
	(n=172)	(162)	(146)	(87)
	%	%	%	%
5 Very positive	15	13	15	13
4	33	33	38	39
3	32	36	34	38
2	15	14	10	9
1 Very negative	5	3	3	1
Don't know/Refused	2	0	1	0

Note: [a]"Using a five-point scale, where 5 is very positive, and 1 is very negative, how would you rate the climate for business and entrepreneurship in your community?" [2]

Table 6.12b: Effectiveness of Economic Development[a] (n=1,122)

Response	Number of Employees			
	1–10	**11–19**	**20–49**	**50–100**
	(n=322)	(314)	(296)	(190)
	%	%	%	%
5 Very effective	11	14	10	13
4	22	26	27	30
3	31	32	33	33
2	20	16	20	16
1 Very ineffective	15	12	10	8
Don't know/Refused	1	0	1	0

Note: [a]"Using a five-point scale, where "5" is very effective, and "1" is very ineffective, how would you rate the economic development efforts in your community?" [3]

Table 6.13b: Major Problems for Starting a Business[a] (n=567)

Response	Yes	No	DK
	%	%	%
Cost of health care			
1–10 employees (n=172)	84	16	0
11–19 employees (n=162)	83	17	1
20–49 employees (n=146)	78	21	1
50–100 employees (n=87)	77	22	1
State and local taxes			
1–10 employees	62	38	–
11–19 employees	70	30	–
20–49 employees	62	38	–
50–100 employees	74	26	–
Poor economic conditions			
1–10 employees	50	50	0
11–19 employees	40	60	0
20–49 employees	33	66	1
50–100 employees	29	71	0
Finding workers			
1–10 employees	48	52	–
11–19 employees	61	39	–
20–49 employees	57	43	–
50–100 employees	47	53	–
A negative climate for business			
1–10 employees	38	62	0
11–19 employees	36	64	1
20–49 employees	32	67	1
50–100 employees	26	74	0

Note: [a]"Which of the following do you think is a major problem or challenge in Nebraska that prevents people from starting a business? Please respond by saying 'yes' or 'no'." [2]

Table 6.14b: Perception of New Competing Business[a] (n=1,122)

Response	Number of Employees			
	1–10	**11–19**	**20–49**	**50–100**
	(n=322)	(314)	(296)	(190)
	%	%	%	%
5 Very positive	15	14	17	19
4	20	25	28	31
3	35	39	36	29
2	18	12	13	12
1 Very negative	11	10	7	9
Don't know/Refused	1	0	0	0

Note: [a]"A business wants to come into your community, but it would compete with several existing businesses. Using a five-point scale, where 5 is very positive, and 1 is very negative, how positive or negative is this development?" [3]

Table 6.15b: Years to Exit Business[a] (n=1,122)

Response	Number of Employees			
	1–10	**11–19**	**20–49**	**50–100**
	(n=322)	(314)	(296)	(190)
	%	%	%	%
0–5 years	28	25	23	30
6–10	24	27	28	24
11–15	9	13	17	12
More than 15 years	29	27	24	23
Don't know/Refused	10	8	7	11

Note: [a]"In how many years do you plan to exit your business?" [3]

Table 6.16b: Who to Transfer Business to[a] (n=1,122)

Response	Number of Employees			
	1–10	**11–19**	**20–49**	**50–100**
	(n=322)	(314)	(296)	(190)
	%	%	%	%
Family	36	35	35	31
Employee(s)	8	18	20	20
Third party	18	26	26	30
Liquidate	26	12	8	10
Other	3	3	5	2
Don't know/Refused	8	7	7	9

Note: [a]"Who do you plan on transferring your business to?" [3]

APPENDIX 6C: Nebraska vs. United States Data

Table 6.1c: Government Regulation of Business[a]

Response	General Public		Business Owners	
	Nebr.	U.S.	Nebr.	U.S.
	(n=4,935)	(607)	(1,122)	(403)
	%	%	%	%
Too much government regulation	59	50	70	56
Too little government regulation	8	12	4	7
About the right amount of government regulation	29	34	25	32
Don't know/Refused	6	5	1	5

Note: [a]"Thinking about government regulation of business, do you think there is:" [3]

Table 6.3c: Business Taxes[a]

Response	General Public		Business Owners	
	Nebr.	U.S.	Nebr.	U.S.
	(n=4,935)	(607)	(1,122)	(403)
	%	%	%	%
Overtaxed	42	46	64	71
Undertaxed	17	15	6	4
Taxed about the right amount	37	32	29	22
Don't know/Refused	7	7	3	3

Note: [a]"Thinking about taxes, do you think that most businesses are:" [3]

Table 6.9c: Importance of Community Contribution[a]

Response	General Public		Business Owners	
	Nebr.	U.S.	Nebr.	U.S.
	(n=4,935)	(607)	(567)	(403)
	%	%	%	%
5 Very important	51	57	48	48
4	29	24	30	23
3	14	11	17	22
2	4	3	3	4
1 Not at all important	2	4	2	3
Don't know/Refused	1	2	1	1

Note: [a]"Using a five-point scale, where '5' is very important, and '1' is not at all important, how important do you think it is for successful business owners or entrepreneurs to contribute something to the community beyond providing jobs or paying taxes?" [3]

Table 6.10c: Motivations for Community Contribution[a]

Reasons[b]	Major	Minor	Not
	%	%	%
They want to help the community			
Nebraska General Public (n=2,475)	78	18	3
U.S. General Public (n=607)	58	37	5
Nebraska Business Owners (n=567)	78	19	2
U.S. Business Owners (n=403)	73	24	3
They want to promote their business			
Nebraska General Public	75	20	2
U.S. General Public	85	12	3
Nebraska Business Owners	74	23	2
U.S. Business Owners	75	22	3
It is tax deductible			
Nebraska General Public	49	39	8
U.S. General Public	60	32	7
Nebraska Business Owners	42	44	13
U.S. Business Owners	38	49	13

Notes:
[a]"For each of the possible reasons a business owner or entrepreneur might have for contributing to the community beyond providing jobs or paying taxes, do you think it would be a major reason, a minor reason, or not a reason at all?" [2]
[b]Don't know responses were omitted in the table.

CHAPTER 7

Actions to Advance
Entrepreneurship in Nebraska

The analysis of economic data and the survey results has shown that Nebraska is an entrepreneurial state. Nebraska was in the middle of the pack among states on the State Entrepreneurship Index. The survey analysis of Nebraska households and business owners indicated a significant interest in entrepreneurship in Nebraska and respect for the role entrepreneurs play in the economy and larger society.

The citizens of Nebraska should be pleased that the state has achieved a moderate level of entrepreneurship rather than a low level. Entrepreneurship is critical for the continual improvement in the state's economy. It contributes to such positive forces as economic growth, productivity, job creation, business diversity, and philanthropy, all of which enrich and revitalize the state in many ways. A poor climate for entrepreneurship, by contrast, reduces the prospects for economic growth, job creation, and the other factors that contribute to the state's development. With this decline in entrepreneurship come diminished expectations and aspirations across the state. This condition becomes a significant barrier to future prosperity.

In spite of its moderate ranking, there is ample reason to work to improve the entrepreneurial climate in the state. First, Nebraska operates in a competitive environment within the country, in constant competition with other states for resources, capital, and people. And, as was explained in previous chapters, entrepreneurship is playing an increasingly large role in the economy, given growing levels of self-employment and business formation. Participants in all sectors of the state's economy and leaders from all major institutions within Nebraska need to find ways to increase the entrepreneurial activity in the state just to maintain our current position compared with other states.

Second, there is reason to believe that the state could move up in the rankings to become one of the more entrepreneurial states in the nation. Although this outcome may seem distant, it is worth noting that other smaller states in this area of the country, such as Utah and Idaho, have become highly ranked entrepreneurial states. Over time, Nebraska has the opportunity to become one of the leaders in entrepreneurship among states.

Third, technology gives firms greater flexibility in location. Firms based in small communities can serve customers throughout the nation and the world, and utilize a far flung network of suppliers and contractors. Nebraskans living in small towns and cities have the potential to create rapidly growing firms of national scope.   States like Nebraska with a significant rural population are not disadvantaged in entrepreneurship.

This chapter discusses actions that can be taken to develop such an entrepreneurial climate in Nebraska at both the state level and in local communities within the state. The concept of improving the entrepreneurial climate in Nebraska is a broad-based one that will involve many people throughout the state working individually or in groups through organizations and institutions. The main objective is to design actions that work on many margins to improve the opportunities for entrepreneurs and the prospects for business success. Although it is true that entrepreneurs are problem solvers who can survive even in a challenging business environment, the goal is to create a climate for entrepreneurship in Nebraska that helps more business ventures get launched, fosters their development, and encourages them to remain in the state.

ACTION SET

What actions can be taken? The possibilities are endless and only limited by the imagination and resource constraints. It is simply not possible to list in detail the full array of the possible choice sets or describe in detail how each activity should be undertaken to achieve the desired goals or objectives for expanding entrepreneurship in Nebraska. There needs to be more discussion and analysis by the individuals, groups, and organizations in all sectors of the state's economy before a desired choice set of actions is identified and work is undertaken to implement actions that can make a significant contribution to improving the entrepreneurial climate.

To encourage this process, we outline a set of potential actions. The set is by no means exhaustive and is offered in the spirit of providing structure and focus. The concern is that without it the discussion can easily go in diverse directions and result in no worthwhile actions being undertaken by any party. Opinions about how best to advance entrepreneurship in the state often differ because people approach the topic from individual perspectives and from particular vantage points of personal interest. The encouragement of entrepreneurship, however, is a more complex and subtle process with multiple perspectives. Table 7.1 presents three major ones and their subsets, each of which merits further explanation.

Table 7.1: Three Perspectives on Promoting Entrepreneurship

Increasing the supply of entrepreneurs and their support
- A. Entrepreneurship education
- B. Business succession and transfer

Expanding access to technology and capital
- A. Technology transfer
- B. Angel investors
- C. Entrepreneurship endowment
- D. Technical support

Improving the business climate for entrepreneurs
- A. Taxes
- B. Regulation
- C. Health care
- D. Quality of life

The first perspective covers actions that influence the "supply" of entrepreneurs among a state's existing population, both as an inflow and an outflow. On the inflow side, this work would involve increasing the number of people who are seriously considering the launching of entrepreneurial ventures, primarily through education, but also through other training avenues. On the outflow side, business succession needs to be addressed. In many communities across the state, especially in rural areas, there is concern about from where the new entrepreneurs who will take over and improve existing businesses when the current owners retire will come.

A second perspective focuses on actions designed to enhance access to critical resources for entrepreneurship, such as capital or technology. The issues in this dimension include ones that have been widely discussed nationwide, but they deserve more consideration in Nebraska. There is the need to expand venture capital funding or angel investing in the state so that new firms have more access to capital and mentoring. With the expansion of university research, more opportunities exist for technological transfers from this research to commercial ventures. And as the number of start-ups in the state expands, they will increase the demand for technical or professional assistance from service providers in the private sector.

The third perspective focuses on business issues that affect the economic climate in Nebraska. Such issues include taxes, government regulation, the provision of health care, and quality of life, to name some major ones that affect existing and new businesses. As noted previously, entrepreneurs are expert at overcoming obstacles, so it is unclear whether concerns about these issues actually prevent individuals from starting businesses. With that point made, however, it should also be noted that serial entrepreneurs – those individuals who repeatedly start and sell businesses – may be quite sensitive to business climate issues, and prefer to move their existing businesses and wealth to a state with a more favorable environment. Burdensome taxes and regulation may cause a state to lose too many of its serial entrepreneurs.

The development of the three perspectives and their subsets for expanding entrepreneurship in Nebraska came from several sources of inspiration. We began the work by studying the academic research into the foundations of entrepreneurship and the financing of new business ventures. We then reviewed some of the existing programs and projects in Nebraska and other states that are designed to aid entrepreneurs and stimulate business.

Perhaps the most important activity we undertook to enrich our understanding was a series of extensive interviews we conducted with many Nebraskans on the topic of entrepreneurship. The purpose of the interviews was to provide a "real world" context for the knowledge we gained in our academic study and program review. We spoke with entrepreneurs who had started their own businesses in different industries. We had conversations with business leaders and executives working in the finance, legal, marketing, and real estate professions that provide key services to small and growing businesses. We had discussions with education leaders and government officials to get their views of what should and could be done. Taken together, the interviews and other conversations we had gave us significant new insights about the dynamics of entrepreneurship in the state and substantially shaped our conceptions of the multiple perspectives for entrepreneurship.

With this background, we can now turn to a fuller discussion of the potential actions for encouraging entrepreneurship in Nebraska. The primary goal is to present a menu of the approaches. No specific actions or policies are recommended, however, because what may work for the state or a local community will vary and often depend on fiscally feasibility. We also do not focus on current public or private programs to stimulate entrepreneurship in Nebraska. A few interesting examples are cited, but there is no attempt to identify or assess all projects. The main purpose is to describe the possible actions that may enhance entrepreneurship, and thus contribute to economic development and an improved quality of life in Nebraska.

We also emphasize actions that facilitate entrepreneurship in businesses both large and small, and in a variety of industries. We see great promise in increasing both the number of "lifestyle" businesses that primarily provide a living for the owner and a few employees and "high-growth" businesses that create dozens or even hundreds of jobs. Growth in the number of smaller, lifestyle businesses can provide more Nebraska citizens with the satisfaction and independence offered by business ownership. Further, as we envision entrepreneurship as a career, we anticipate transitions between lifestyle and high-growth entrepreneurship. Individuals who may begin their careers by starting lifestyle businesses may develop skills that allow them to develop high-growth businesses in the future.

SUPPLY OF ENTREPRENEURS

As the results from the Gallup surveys show, there is no single path to entrepreneurship. Some people are drawn to entrepreneurship by a desire to create something new, or to be self-directed by being their own boss. Other individuals benefit from a family history in business ownership that provides them with business mentors and a rich education in the practices of business owners. Other entrepreneurs started a business out of necessity because they lost a job when their employer downsized, sold, or closed the business.

These varied paths to entrepreneurship demonstrate that there is no single policy to enact that can significantly increase the supply of entrepreneurs. Entrepreneurs tend to supply themselves for a variety of reasons. There may, however, be several actions that can be taken to increase the supply of potential entrepreneurs in Nebraska either by using education to increase the flow of people into entrepreneurship or by developing practices for business succession that reduce the outflow from entrepreneurship.

Education

Entrepreneurship education can increase the number of young people who envision themselves starting a business at some point in their lives and have some of the information, skills, and experience required to start and maintain a business when they decide to undertake the challenge. Such actions in this area may include educational programs and experiences for students to learn important entrepreneurial skills and expertise. This education needs to come at a relatively young age. As has been cited in the survey findings from business owners in Nebraska, the idea of becoming an entrepreneur often comes when people are younger, although the act to become an entrepreneur may not be taken until later in life.   Early education and exposure to entrepreneurship creates more job and career possibilities in the future.[1]

To increase the supply of potential entrepreneurs there needs to be an organized effort to educate students in elementary and secondary schools, community colleges, and universities.   The educational programs for entrepreneurship include general curricula to teach all students business knowledge and skills. They can also include specific mentoring or internship experiences for developing and operating a small business. Although the latter programs offer intensive training for a limited number of students, they increase the likelihood that students, at some time in the future, would pursue an entrepreneurial venture at some point in their lives.

The advantages of increasing entrepreneurship education can be demonstrated with use of some of the survey results. One item on the general public survey showed that about seven in ten (69%) young adults in Nebraska, ages 18 to 29, expressed interest in starting a business (Table 4.1). Among this group about half stated that they were likely or very likely to act on this idea (Table 4.2). A cross-tabulation of the two results means that over a third (35%) of young adults in Nebraska are both interested in starting a business and say they are likely or very likely to do so. These results mean that for every 10,000 young adults in this age group, there are about 3,500 potential entrepreneurs in Nebraska.   Additional education and training is likely to increase this pool of potential entrepreneurs.

This increase in turn can affect the number of Nebraskans who decide to become an entrepreneur. A national study in 2006 found that about 0.28 percent of the adult population (those ages 20 to 64 and who did not already own a business) created new businesses each month in Nebraska.[2] These numbers mean that 28 out of every 10,000 Nebraskans create a business each month. The average for the nation is 29 per 10,000 adults creating new businesses per month. It ranges from a low of 16 to a high of 60 adults per 10,000 adults.   It would not take a large increase in the number of entrepreneurs per 10,000 adults in Nebraska to improve significantly the entrepreneurial activity in the state.   This increase can come from the increased pool of potential entrepreneurs created by educational initiatives.

The value of more entrepreneurship education is not just about creating start-ups. The skills, knowledge, and mindset that comes from learning about entrepreneurship, together with how business and the economy work, is important for all students and at all levels of education regardless of their career paths. Not all students will become entrepreneurs, but all students will benefit from knowing more about the process because in a dynamic economy, everyone needs to be more entrepreneurial at whatever job they hold in the private, public, or non-profit sector. This knowledge and appreciation of entrepreneurship creates a business climate that is more supportive by the greater population of the few who are willing to accept the significant risks and sacrifices that are associated with business ownership and development.

Nebraska has an active system of business education in many school districts, which is where entrepreneurship is traditionally taught.[3] This education typically begins in middle or high schools as a course or unit of instruction in the business education curriculum. The course or unit is generally taken as an elective, and it is not often a requirement for college admission. As a consequence, few high school students take such a course or unit, or receive a sound education in entrepreneurship before they graduate.

To address some of these concerns, the Lincoln Public Schools developed an innovative entrepreneurship focus program for high school students in 2006.[4] The program has a total enrollment of about 80 students a year. To be admitted to the program, students apply from schools across the district. If admitted, they spend part of their instructional day taking courses in subjects such as math, English, business education, or economics that have an entrepreneurship theme. Other activities include internships, a speaker series featuring entrepreneurs, business plan development, student competitions, and student-directed learning. The program partners with the Lincoln business community, Gallup, Southeast Community College (SCC), and the University of Nebraska-Lincoln among other entities. Information on this high school program has been shared with other school districts in the state to encourage its adoption by them.

At the community college level, entrepreneurship education is widely available through business administration departments. For example, students enrolled in SCC can earn an associate of applied science degree with a focus on entrepreneurship.[5] The other five community colleges in the Nebraska have, or are developing, a similar entrepreneurial focus in their business administration curriculum for students taking business courses. As a result of these activities, students throughout the state have the opportunity to develop entrepreneurship skills from high school through community college.

Public universities in Nebraska also offer coursework in entrepreneurship for those students seeking a four-year undergraduate degree. For example, the College of Business Administration at the University of Nebraska-Lincoln offers nearly a dozen undergraduate and graduate courses on entrepreneurship and related topics through its Center for Entrepreneurship and management department.

This brief review shows that entrepreneurship education is available for the most part in Nebraska at all levels for those students who want to pursue it. Nothing in the review, however, is meant to imply that the system is highly efficient or productive in developing graduates who become Nebraska entrepreneurs. That subject has not been given extensive study as far as we are aware. There may be inefficiencies in the system, because of the problems with accepting college credit at different institutions or because of competition among educational institutions, which limits the number of graduates with entrepreneurship training. There also may be ways to increase the flow of students to such programs, and thus increase their productivity, once a student enters a course of study in entrepreneurship.

One new entrepreneurship initiative at the University of Nebraska-Lincoln is to expand the entrepreneurship education outside of the College of Business Administration to encompass all areas of the university including arts and humanities and engineering. The goal is to encourage more students in other fields of study to consider entrepreneurship for employment in addition to wage or salary employment. This initiative raises the point that educational institutions can move beyond enrollment in entrepreneurship focus programs and majors to encouraging all students to see themselves as entrepreneurs. Schools and colleges offer general education, but they also are designed to train students in particular occupations and professions, most likely for wage and salary work, at least early in their careers. Schools, advisors, and counselors often help students identify majors and professions.

One point consistently made by the entrepreneurs we interviewed is that they received little encouragement to pursue a career in entrepreneurship during their education. This raises the question of what, besides programs and curricula, can high schools or colleges and universities do to encourage students, when appropriate, to consider entrepreneurship as a job or career path. One step would be to help teachers, as part of their own continuing education, to recognize the traits of potential entrepreneurs to identify students with potential for that career. Guidance counselors also could receive training in identifying students with the greatest potential for entrepreneurship, or perhaps just as importantly, great potential for success in entrepreneurship relative to their potential in other professions or skilled work. College and university faculty members and advisors also need to give more information to students about this entrepreneurship option when discussing career options or job prospects.

Business Succession and Transfer

When business owners want to retire, they may prefer that a close family member or relative purchases or takes over the business. The family member or relative may not have become a business owner under other circumstances, but may enter a career of entrepreneurship through business succession. Actions that increase the efficiency and feasibility of business succession, as opposed to the closing of the business, its sale to an existing entrepreneur, or the slow decay of the business because the existing owner wants to retire, may increase the supply of entrepreneurs in the Nebraska economy. These business owners may not only maintain the existing enterprises, but based on their experience, they may open other businesses in the future.

One major concern for family members or relatives taking over a business is the financing. This financing issue is made all the more complicated by the inheritance tax. There needs to be a tax policy on inheriting a business that reduces the complications and increases the rewards for assuming this responsibility. The inheritance tax can create high demands for cash to settle tax liability and thus result in encouraging or necessitating the sale or liquidation of a family business. The state of Nebraska recently addressed its own inheritance tax to correct some of these problems. The major burden of the inheritance tax, however, is at the federal level. More work needs to be done within the state to focus attention on this problem at the federal level because the inheritance tax can adversely affect the continuation and expansion of entrepreneurship in Nebraska.

There are resources to help with some aspects of business succession. In particular, there is a well-established service and consulting industry available to work with business owners on the legal and financial aspects of transferring a family business. The business can be taken over by family members or relatives, or perhaps a party connected to the owner through employment or friendship. In either case, the main concern is to attract young adults in accepting this challenge because they have many interesting job alternatives available to them that can pay a good wage or salary, especially if they have a college education or good skill set. There is a need to identify and pursue actions that will make taking over a family business a satisfying and rewarding choice for these individuals.

Young adults are often concerned about finding satisfying jobs or careers with opportunities to influence businesses, to devise creative solutions to problems, and to gain a sense of accomplishment. Entrepreneurship offers such job and career satisfaction, and as such it needs to be promoted among young adults. In this respect, networking, peer relationships, and information can be used. Local organizations such as chambers of commerce or young entrepreneur clubs could make an effort to involve the next generation of potential owners of family businesses, as well as the current owners, in their functions. Their inclusion in informational events, task forces, and other programs would allow a new generation to see some of the opportunities to influence the community that come with business ownership. Furthermore, potential successors need more chances to meet other young people who have taken over family businesses, thrived by building the businesses, and taken them in new directions after succession.

In this respect, there may be a role for local institutions, such as the University Extension Service, to work with family-owned businesses on the non-financial aspects of transition. The University of Minnesota, for example, as part of its *Rural Minnesota Life* initiative, has a series of tools to provide education and training for family business succession. These tools help families consider how to begin the transfer of management authority to the next generation of business owners.

Business succession also can help increase the number of entrepreneurs in Nebraska towns and cities by attracting other new entrepreneurs who are not associated with a business owner. There needs to be an expansion of programs that recruit the new entrepreneurs to take over existing businesses in communities across the state. Such efforts, at least indirectly, are already underway through the recruitment of new working-age residents.

One example is the Norfolk Area Recruiters (NAR) group that was set up to "attract graduates from the Norfolk area to return to the communities that raised them."[6] Through its website, the NAR advertises job opportunities available in the community, including a posting of businesses for sale.[7] This volunteer group, which is funded by the City of Norfolk and donations by local businesses and individuals, also contacts individuals who register on the website to inform them about opportunities for recreation and community involvement in the area. The group states that it has recruited at least 28 families back to the Norfolk area, and a number of the "success stories" are business owners.[8] These business owners include individuals who have founded new businesses as well as those who have taken over succession businesses.

This recruitment work will be of vital importance to future economic growth in Nebraska. This volunteer activity can expand the supply of future entrepreneurs in communities throughout the state and help address problems of business succession and transfer. More generally, the work shows that sustained local efforts in communities can make a significant difference, and that the responsibility for fostering a positive and inviting climate for entrepreneurship is as much a local issue as it is a state or national one.

CLUSTERS, INVESTORS, AND KNOWLEDGE

Another set of public or private actions to stimulate entrepreneurship involve direct efforts in technology and innovation fields. These actions often come with a focus on encouraging entrepreneurs who create rapidly growing or highly innovative businesses, or serial entrepreneurs who form multiple new businesses. This work forms a cluster of experienced entrepreneurs and managers who can drive the development of new companies in Nebraska that have the potential for high growth. The concentration of these individuals creates a productive environment for high-growth entrepreneurship.

Technology Transfer from Universities

As was noted in Chapter 2, Nebraska has a relatively low level of patents per capita. This suggests that Nebraska is not commercializing new technologies and innovations at the same rate as many states. This lag occurs despite the fact that the state is the location of several universities, including engineering colleges, bio-medical research centers, and two medical schools. Improved commercialization of university research offers a likely avenue in Nebraska to increase its share of high-growth and innovative businesses.

Universities throughout the state have expanded these commercialization efforts in recent years. For example, the Office of Technology Development at the University of Nebraska-Lincoln assists university researchers in disclosing inventions and obtaining patents, developing start-up businesses, or marketing for licensing of new innovations and technologies. Other universities in the state have similar units. The UNeMed provides technology transfer services for the University of Nebraska Medical Center, including the program Advance Nebraska, which gives preferential treatment to Nebraska firms who license from UNeMed. At Creighton University, there is an Office of Technology Transfer to handle inventions or research discoveries that have commercial appeal.

These focused units within a larger university can contribute significantly to the formation of technology-based businesses in Nebraska. This work, however, cannot succeed alone, and depends on the general advancement of technology and innovative business in the state. In particular, research has shown that university progress in patents and licensing can spill over to the local economy only if there is an active local business community in technology industries.[9] If university-based technology transfer programs are to be successful, there needs to be increased development of technology-based entrepreneurship spurred from other private or public sources.

Angel Investors

One such source to spawn more businesses is angel investors. These investors are typically experienced and wealthy entrepreneurs who investigate opportunities to provide funding in early stages of a business. The financing from angel investors fills the gap between the initial self-financing from the entrepreneur, and the later and more sizable financing that comes from venture capitalists. Angels often receive a stake in the new business in return for financing that allows the business to reach commercial scale.

Angel investors typically do not operate alone. They often form groups or networks of entrepreneurs who focus on high-growth or innovative businesses with sound plans for development. Individual members of the network choose whether or not to invest in individual companies to effectively spread the risk among the larger group investors. Angel investor networks often limit the investments to certain areas, such as a particular state or city, or to specific industries, such as computer technology, bio-technology, or health care.

Angel investors have an interest in the economic development of their cities or states, but these investors also have an interest in making profits. An attractive high-risk investment often features an "exit strategy" where business plans call for the eventual sale or licensing of the business to a larger entity. For this reason, angel investor networks also foster the development of infrastructure for serial entrepreneurship within a state. Angels sometimes mentor or counsel the aspiring entrepreneurs, or team the new entrepreneurs with managers experienced with start-ups.

As the activity of angel networks grows, the cluster of serial entrepreneurs and growth managers grows as well. Angel networks have deep roots in California and other centers of entrepreneurship in the United States. Angel networks also are developing in Nebraska. The Nebraska Angels group was founded in 2006.[10] Based on the track record of similar organizations around the nation, entrepreneurship in Nebraska will benefit as more experienced entrepreneurs and investors join this organization or form similar angel organizations in their communities to help fill an important gap in the financing of growing businesses, to provide expertise to new entrepreneurs, and to build the stock of entrepreneurs who also become serial entrepreneurs by starting multiple businesses in the state.

Entrepreneurship Endowment

Angel investor groups have been motivated by community service, providing another example of how private individuals support entrepreneurship. There also are opportunities for private individuals and businesses to make direct investments in start-up firms, or in community organizations that make loans to new businesses. Two advantages of direct investment from private sources should be noted. First, the private sector may be able to provide a larger and steadier source of funding for entrepreneurship. In fact, private donations have been a critical source of revenue for local industrial recruitment organizations for decades. Second, private investors may be more effective in monitoring the performance of local organizations and more flexible in withdrawing funding from ineffective organizations. Given these advantages, the primary role of government would be to provide incentives to encourage private donations and investment.

Kansas provides an ambitious example of promoting private investment to promote entrepreneurship. As part of the 2004 Kansas Economic Growth Act, Kansas provides a 50 percent tax credit on angel investments as part of a program overseen by the Kansas Technology Enterprise Program. Kansas also provides a 50 percent tax credit to individual and corporate donations to a set of regional investment pools run by local organizations.[11] There is state involvement and regulation in this activity because the Kansas Department of Commerce chooses which local organizations will run each regional investment pool. These community investment pools significantly diversify the funds available to entrepreneurs. These pools could loan money to entrepreneurs in the full range of industries. By contrast, angel investor groups tend to focus on investment in firms in technology-based industries, and in businesses that feature a relatively quick "exit strategy."

Nebraska may wish to implement a similar tax credit program. If this type of program is established, the rate of the credit and the number of eligible regional investment pools need careful study and determination. Nebraska may wish to focus on the regional investment pool approach. Angel investors also would benefit from a tax credit, but may prefer to operate without interference from a government program or agency. In any case, any tax credits to angel investor groups should be designed so that there is no interference with the emerging angel groups in Nebraska.

Technical and Professional Assistance

Entrepreneurs often use a variety of professional services when starting their businesses. As businesses grow from self-employment or home operations to more established and larger firms with employees and commercial office space, emerging entrepreneurs require new or expanded services for real estate, accounting, law, insurance, marketing, and technology. New entrepreneurs may be inexperienced about their needs in each area, uncertain both about where to obtain services or how to evaluate their quality.

Entrepreneurs can be expected to find service providers, given that service firms have an incentive to provide these services to paying customers. At the same time, however, new and small businesses are unlikely to be the largest or most important clients of the various service firms. Real estate agents, lawyers, accountants, insurance agents, marketers, or technology specialists may have varying levels of experience or skills in working with the many new businesses they encounter in offering their services.

This situation suggests a role for professional associations at the state or sub-state level to help their membership provide the best possible services to new entrepreneurs. There are at least two types of steps that can be taken. First, professional organizations could provide guidance and materials for new entrepreneurs to help them determine their needs and choose firms with interest and experience in working with new business people. Second, as part of professional training, professional organizations could develop curricula to train their members about best provision of services to new entrepreneurs in local communities.

The efforts to provide specialized services to new entrepreneurs must ultimately be directed by professional organizations in Nebraska that represent the accounting, real estate, legal, insurance, or other professions that offer services of value to the new entrepreneurs. Help also can come from general business service organizations such as chambers of commerce in different communities. Many business associations and chambers of commerce in Nebraska already have in place active programs of this type, so the main recommendation here is that these business associations and organizations revisit the scope of the efforts to see if they can do a better job of helping the new entrepreneur grow a business.

BUSINESS CLIMATE

Business climate refers to the underlying economic conditions affecting business operations in a state or local community. Although many factors affect the business climate, taxes, regulation, health care costs, and the quality of life are key considerations. An unfavorable business climate can drive out economic activity by encouraging resident entrepreneurs, skilled workers, and capital investors to leave the state, and at the same time it discourages anyone outside the state with entrepreneurial intentions, productive work skills, or financial capital to invest in firms from entering the state.

Business climate generally influences business or economic decisions for all private firms, but it can have a significant effect on entrepreneurship. Such a situation would arise if taxes or other costs of doing business in a state fall especially hard on smaller businesses compared with larger businesses, or if taxes or business costs for self-employment were heavier than it would be for wage and salary employment. If business or economic conditions favor large businesses in a state, then fewer of the state's residents would have an economic incentive to pursue entrepreneurship.

Tax Climate

Taxes on income or profits reduce the returns from all types of economic activity including earnings from work as well as profits from self-employment. A weaker business environment reduces all types of business activity including entrepreneurship.[12] At the state and local level, this effect is best understood in terms of out-migration. Higher taxes may drive younger prospective entrepreneurs to pursue their interests in other parts of the country, with a more favorable tax climate. Established entrepreneurs who are not closely tied to the local economy also will have incentive to relocate to areas with a more favorable tax climate.[13]

General reductions in tax rates would aid entrepreneurship in Nebraska by encouraging entrepreneurs to remain in or move into the state. Researchers have found higher taxes discourage entrepreneurship. In particular, higher top income tax rates, higher sales tax rates, and higher inheritance tax rates modestly reduce the share of national entrepreneurship found in a state.[14] Further, a more effective policy to encourage entrepreneurship might be a tax cut or credit targeted at entrepreneurs, especially during the first few years of business operations when revenues and profitability are most uncertain. At the margin, such a tax policy could significantly improve the odds for business success.

Regulatory Climate

Regulations, like taxes, significantly raise the cost of doing business. Regulations therefore reduce the incentives to start businesses, remain in business, or expand employment. The burden on entrepreneurship may be particularly hard if regulatory costs fall disproportionately on smaller businesses. For example, one study found that minimum wage laws discourage entrepreneurship because the burden of this regulation falls especially hard on small and new businesses, and because these firms employ a larger share of minimum wage workers.[15] That outcome can occur if the costs of compliance do not change much with the firm output, so that costs are spread more on a per worker basis for smaller firms.

There are thousands of government rules and regulations that affect business decision making. This number makes it difficult to measure and estimate the impact of regulations in 50 individual states. There have, however, been several attempts to analyze the cost of regulation at the federal level. This research suggests that regulatory costs, particularly environmental and tax compliance regulations fall disproportionately on small businesses.

Several reports of the Small Business Administration define four types of regulation: (1) economic (e.g., trade laws); (2) workplace; (3) environmental; and, (4) tax compliance.[16] Focusing on the most recent report, the average cost of federal regulations per worker was approximately $5,600. Given that the average annual wage of U.S. workers is approximately $30,000, the regulatory cost estimate suggests that federal regulations are about 19 percent of the average wage and significantly add to the cost of doing business. The costs of state and local regulations would only add to this burden. With total regulatory costs of this magnitude, even a small reduction in the regulatory cost burden would be sufficient to influence the location decision of entrepreneurs. The states and local communities with a high regulatory burden would encourage out-migration of its entrepreneurs, and attract fewer entrepreneurs.

The reports also suggest that at the federal level the costs of regulation fall disproportionately on the smallest businesses. Many entrepreneurs run smaller businesses, at least in the initial years of operation. The researchers found that the overall costs of regulation were $7,600 per job for businesses with fewer than 20 employees versus just $5,400 per job for businesses with 20 to 499 employees, and $5,300 per job for firms with 500 or more employees. Much of the difference was due to the higher costs of environmental compliance, though firms with fewer than 20 employees also paid $300 to $500 more per worker for tax compliance.

There are many avenues to reduce the state and local regulatory burden, and such activity should be helpful for entrepreneurship. One approach would be to institute a policy to limit regulation or discourage new regulation. The Small Business Administration recently developed model legislation for states to introduce "regulatory flexibility." The model regulation includes a requirement to conduct an economic impact analysis of all proposed regulations, a regulatory flexibility analysis of all proposed regulations, a guarantee that businesses may request a judicial review of new regulation, and a required periodic review of all existing regulations.[17] Nebraska is one of 11 states without regulatory flexibility legislation or executive order.

Finally, immigration is increasingly a regulatory issue for state and local governments. Many state and local governments have been unsatisfied with federal immigration policy and have been adopting their own policies to address illegal immigration within their borders. Immigration policy has many potential implications for the economy, including entrepreneurship. International migrants start new businesses at a significant rate and legal international migrants can add to the supply of entrepreneurs just like domestic immigrants. State and local governments should make sure that policies designed to reduce illegal immigration do not have the unintended consequence of also significantly reducing legal immigration, or of significantly raising compliance costs for business.[18]

Health Care

Survey work in the last few years has confirmed that health care costs are a key competitive concern of Nebraska businesses.[19] There would be advantages for both workers and business owners if the rate of growth in health care costs could be slowed without discouraging the new treatments continuously being developed by our nation's innovative health care industry.

Health care delivery and costs are a complex issue, influencing different sectors of the economy, including small business and entrepreneurship. In particular, one key issue influencing the supply of entrepreneurs in the economy is the relatively high cost of health care coverage for small businesses. Larger purchasing groups, such as large employers, are able to obtain insurance at lower rates. This discrepancy means that individuals considering entrepreneurship may face higher health care costs by forming their own businesses rather than remaining with a larger employer. This cost disadvantage will not discourage many potential entrepreneurs, but for some aspiring entrepreneurs this additional cost could be the difference between becoming an entrepreneur or remaining with wage and salary employment.[20]

There are many actions that can be taken to reduce health care costs for entrepreneurs. One method is for firms to band together into groups to purchase health insurance, as is often done through business associations. Chambers of commerce and local economic developers pool groups of small businesses to purchase insurance and realize some of the costs savings of larger firms. Some chambers of commerce in Nebraska are already offering these programs. Other states have made efforts to reduce health care costs by lowering medical malpractice costs for health care providers.

Quality of Life

One researcher argues that a key to entrepreneurship is the cultivation of a "creative class." The concept does not refer to individuals with substantial human capital, but to those with a creative orientation, and a proclivity towards entrepreneurship. In this view, entrepreneurship is one manifestation of creativity, and thrives in places that encourage of creativity and diversity. Such places can more easily attract and retain a creative class.[21]

This approach emphasizes fostering a creative climate in states and locales rather than simply emphasizing the need for a positive business climate. More specific policy implications are to focus on building the quality of place in regions through the built environment, encouragement of culture and arts, and quality of life amenities. Tolerance for individuals of different races, national origins, and lifestyles also is an emphasis of this strategy.

The support for this approach comes from a correlation between multiple indexes of creativity and tolerance and the incidence of high-technology entrepreneurship. What is not clear from the research is whether this correlation reflects any sort of causality. While the factors may be correlated, creativity and tolerance may not on their own cause high-technology entrepreneurship. It is equally plausible that the presence of high-technology entrepreneurship and the resulting regional growth attracts and retains a more diverse and tolerant population. Alternatively, both may be caused by a third factor, such as a high quality of life in a region.

The key point is that building local quality of life amenities, expanding culture and the arts, improving education, and encouraging creative industries may aid in encouraging entrepreneurship in communities. Further, the growth of an increasingly diverse population in terms of race, national origin, and lifestyle might be seen as a contributor to state and local economic progress rather than a drain on resources or a liability. What this realization means is that actions and policies that enhance the quality of life in states and communities also are likely to influence entrepreneurship.

CONCLUSION

This chapter identified and discussed a range of possible approaches that can be implemented to encourage entrepreneurship within Nebraska. Table 7.2 lists a summary of these possible actions and providers. [22]

Table 7.2: List of Potential Actions to Promote Entrepreneurship

Action	Provider
Increase the supply of potential entrepreneurs	
A. Entrepreneurship education	
1: Provide entrepreneurship curricula	Secondary and post-secondary schools
2: Identify students with entrepreneurial potential	Primary and secondary schools
B. Encouraging business succession	
1: Increase interest in family business	Chambers of commerce; Young entrepreneurs groups
2: Recruit new entrepreneurs	Community organizations
Advance Technology and Capital Formation	
A. Technology transfer	
Transfer inventions to local firms	Public and private universities
B. Angel investors	
Identify, fund, and advise high-growth firms	Experienced entrepreneurs and investors
C. Entrepreneurship endowment	
Private investment in funds loaning money to and advising start-up firms	Private firms and individuals; State government tax credits
D. Technical support	
Professional services for start-up firms	State accounting, legal, and real estate organizations
Improve the Business Climate	
A. Taxes	
Reduce state tax rates	State government
B. Regulation	
Adopt U.S. Small Business Administration regulatory flexibility legislation	State government
C. Health care	
1: Insurance pools for small firms	Chambers of commerce
2: Reduce malpractice costs	State government
D. Quality of life	
Improve amenities and recreation	Private firms and individuals

These suggested actions are meant to be a menu. Private and public groups in the state may wish to implement different strategies at different points in time and regions of the state may develop different priorities for action. There are undoubtedly many other good ideas that we did not cover in the chapter. The key point is that the state, and regions of the state, may wish to benchmark progress in implementing plans for encouraging entrepreneurship, one, two, five, or ten years into the future. Areas should also consider benchmarking the outcome, such as the growth in entrepreneurial activity, and attitudes about entrepreneurship, in future years, so that progress can be measured.

NOTES

1. For a discussion of the benefits of early education in entrepreneurship for high school students and national results from survey studies, see the *Entrepreneur in Youth* (Kourilsky and Walstad 2007).
2. See Fairlie 2007. For a copy of the report, see:
   http://www.kauffman.org/pdf/kiea_62907.pdf
3. For more information on curriculum and instruction for entrepreneurship education, business education, or career education in the Nebraska go to:
   http://www.nde.state.ne.us/entreped/;
   http://www.nde.state.ne.us/BMIT/index.htm.
4. For a full description, see: http://eship.lps.org/index.html.
5. SCC encourages students enrolled in the entrepreneurship focus high school in LPS to continue their entrepreneurship education at SCC by offering dual course credit for selected entrepreneurship courses that are taught at the focus high school.
6. Norfolk Area Recruiters Group 2007. See http://www.norfolkarea.org for additional information.
7. A review of these businesses shows that nearly all indicate the business is for sale because the owner is seeking to retire.
8. Wees, 2007.
9. Jaffe, 1989; Jaffe, Trajtenberg, and Henderson, 1993.
10. See http://www.nebraskaangels.org/home.php for more information on Nebraska Angels, Inc.
11. Private individuals and businesses also may receive a 50 percent tax credit by making donations to the Kansas Community Entrepreneurship Fund. This fund then distributes resources to the local and regional development organizations.
12. Brown et al. (2002) demonstrate that both labor and capital decline in states with higher taxes and higher levels of public services.

13. Another issue is whether the burden of taxes falls excessively onto entrepreneurs, and changes the incentives for self-employment versus wage and salary employment. There has been extensive research on the impact of taxes on the choice between wage and salary employment and self-employment. For example, Bruce (2000) found that higher taxes actually raised the likelihood of changing from wage and salary into self-employment. Bruce (2002) also found that higher taxes had no effect on the probability of exiting self-employment back into wage and salary employment.

14. Bruce and Deskins 2006.

15. Garrett and Wall 2005.

16. Crain, 2005; Crain and Hopkins 2001.

17. See www.sba.gov/advo/laws/law_modelleg.html.

18. An example is the "Oklahoma Taxpayer and Citizen Protection Act of 2007 (HB1804)." The act has many components related to the provision of public services, but aspects of the act also impact employment law. First, employers doing business with local or state public agencies are required to use either the status verifications systems of the U.S. Department of Homeland Security or the U.S. Social Security Administration, or to conduct a criminal background check to determine the legal status of new employees. Second, for all employers, it is illegal for employers to discharge an employee who is a citizen or legal resident while retaining employees whom the employer knows, or should have known, are illegal residents. The first part of the act may be an example of a regulation that does not impose high costs or risk onto employers, while the second may be an example of a regulation that does. See: http://www.okhouse.gov for further information about House Bill 1804.

19. See Table 6.13. Thompson and Sainath (2005) also discuss this issue.

20. For example, Wellington (2001) finds that individuals with access to larger group insurance coverage rates through their spouses were significantly more likely to be self-employed, particularly individuals over the age of 40 years. He estimates reducing the burden of health care costs for entrepreneurs could increase the share of U.S. workers who are self-employed by at least 3 percent.

21. Richard Florida 2002.

22. The programs discussed in this chapter or providers listed in Table 7.2 are far from comprehensive. Many other valuable programs were not featured in this chapter because these efforts are well-known and already established. For example, the Small Business Development Centers of Nebraska make a contribution to encouraging entrepreneurship in the state. The Krieger Family Foundation provides a list of resources to entrepreneurs in Nebraska and in Nebraska community college districts through its web site, www.nebraskaentrepreneur.com.

References

Acs, Z.J., and C. Armington (2004), "Employment growth and entrepreneurial activity in cities," *Regional Studies*, **38**(8), 911–927.

Almeida, P. (1999), "Semiconductor startups and the exploration of new technological territory," in Z.J. Acs (ed.), *Are Small Firms Important? Their Role and Impact* (Chapter 3), Norwell, Massachusetts: Kluwer Academic Publishers.

Beacon Hill Institute 2006, *State Competitiveness Report 2006*, Boston, Massachusetts: Beacon Hill Institute.

Brown, S.P.A., K.J. Hayes, and L.L. Taylor (2003), "State and local policy, factor markets, and regional growth," *The Review of Regional Studies*, **33**(1), 40–60.

Bruce, D. (2000), "Effects of the United States tax system on transitions into self-employment," *Labour Economics* **7**(5), 545–574.

Bruce, D. (2002), "Taxes and entrepreneurial endurance: Evidence from the self-employed," *National Tax Journal* **55**(1), 5–24.

Bruce, D., and J. Deskins (2006), *State Tax Policy and Entrepreneurial Activity*, Small Business Research Summary Number 284 (November), Washington, DC: U.S. Small Business Administration Office of Advocacy.

Carlsson, B. (1999), "Small business, entrepreneurship, and industry dynamics," in Z.J. Acs (ed.), *Are Small Firms Important? Their Role and Impact* (Chapter 6), Norwell, Massachusetts: Kluwer Academic Publishers.

Crain, W.M. (2005), *The Impact of Regulatory Costs on Small Firms*, Report of the U.S. Small Business Administration Office of Advocacy. SHBQ-03-M-0522 (September), Washington, DC: U.S. SBA Office of Advocacy.

Crain, W.M., and T. Hopkins (2001), *The Impact of Regulator Costs on Small Firms*, Report of the U.S. Small Business Administration Office of Advocacy, Washington, DC: U.S. SBA Office of Advocacy.

Edward Lowe Foundation 2006, *The Entrepreneurial Score Card for Michigan*, Big Rock Valley, Michigan: The Edward Lowe Foundation.

Fairlie, R.W. (2007), *Kauffman Index of Entrepreneurial Activity: National Report, 1996–2007*, Kansas City, Missouri: Ewing Marion Kauffman Foundation.

Florida, R. (2002), *The Rise of the Creative Class: And How It's Transforming Work, Leisure, Community, and Everyday Life*, New York: Basic Books.

Florida, R. (2003), "Entrepreneurship, creativity, and regional growth," in D.M. Hart (ed.), *The Emergence of Entrepreneurship Policy: Governance, Start-Ups, and Growth in the U.S. Knowledge Economy* (Chapter 3, 39–58), New York, USA, and Melbourne, Australia: Cambridge University Press.

Garrett, T., and H. Wall (2005), *Creating a Policy Environment for Entrepreneurs*, Federal Reserve Bank of St. Louis Working Paper, 2005-064A, St. Louis, Missouri: Federal Reserve Bank of St. Louis.

Haltiwanger, J., and C.J. Krizan (1999), "Small business and job creation in the United States: The role of new and young business," in Z.J. Acs (ed.), *Are Small Firms Important? Their Role and Impact* (Chapter 5), Norwell, Massachusetts: Kluwer Academic Publishers.

Jaffe, A. (1989), "The real effects of academic research," *American Economic Review.* **79**(5), 957–970.

Jaffe, A., M. Trajtenberg, and R. Henderson (1993), "Geographic Localization of Knowledge Spillovers as Evidenced by Patent Citation," *Quarterly Journal of Economics*, **108**(3), 577–598.

Kourilsky, M.L., and W.B. Walstad (1998a), "Entrepreneurial attitudes and knowledge of black youth," *Entrepreneurship: Theory and Practice*, **23**(2), (Winter), 5–18.

Kourilsky, M.L., and W.B. Walstad (1998b), "Entrepreneurship and female youth: Knowledge, attitudes, gender differences, and educational practices," *Journal of Business Venturing*, **13**(1), 77–88.

Kourilsky, M.L., and W.B. Walstad (2000a), *The "E" Generation: Prepared for the Entrepreneurial Economy?*, Dubuque, Iowa: Kendall/Hunt.

Kourilsky, M.L., and W.B. Walstad (2002), "The early environment and schooling experiences of high-technology entrepreneurs: Insights for entrepreneurship education," *International Journal of Entrepreneurship Education*, **1**(1), 87–106.

Kourilsky, M.L., and W.B. Walstad (2005), *The New Female Entrepreneur: Creating and Sharing the Wealth*, Dubuque, Iowa: Kendall/Hunt.

Kourilsky, M.L., and W.B. Walstad (2007), *The Entrepreneur in Youth: An Untapped Resource for Economic Growth, Social Entrepreneurship, and Education*, Cheltenham, U.K. and Northampton, Massachusetts: Edward Elgar.

Low, S., J. Henderson, and S. Weiler (2005), "Gauging a Region's Entrepreneurial Potential," in *Economic Review*, **90**(3) (Third Quarter), Kansas City, MO: Federal Reserve Bank of Kansas City, 61–89.

Norfolk Area Recruiters (NAR) (2007), www.norfolkarea.org.

Sainath, J., and Thompson, E. (2005), "Business priorities for reducing the cost of doing business in Nebraska," *Business in Nebraska*, **60**(679), (March), 1–4.

Schramm, C.J. (2006), *The Entrepreneurial Imperative: How America's Miracle Will Reshape the World (and Change Your Life)*, New York: HarperCollins.

U.S. Small Business Administration, Office of Advocacy (2007), State Regulatory Activity Fact Sheet, www.sba.gov/advo/laws/law_modelleg.html.

Walstad, W.B., and M.L. Kourilsky (1996), "The findings from a national survey of entrepreneurship and small business," *Journal of Private Enterprise*, **11**(2), (Spring), 21–32.

Walstad, W.B., and M.L. Kourilsky (1999), *Seeds of Success: Entrepreneurship and Youth*, Dubuque, Iowa: Kendall/Hunt.

Wees, G. (2007), "Recruiters want to hire a full time coordinator," *Norfolk Daily News*, (October 2).

Wellington, A. (2001), "Health insurance coverage and entrepreneurship," *Contemporary Economic Policy*, **19**(4), 465–478.

Index